THE REGIMENT
THE TRUE STORY OF THE SAS / BOOK 1

SCRIPT
Vincent Brugeas

ARTWORK
Thomas Legrain

COLOURS
Elvire De Cock

CINEBOOK
The 9th Art Publisher

It would be daft to think anyone can write a book on his own – let alone a comic. Therefore, I must thank for this album:
Gauthier, for trusting me from the very beginning of this adventure.
Thomas, for his earnestness, dedication, and demanding nature. Those are the qualities from which beautiful albums are born.
Elvire for her 50 shades of desert.
Camille, Charlotte, Diane, and the whole team at Le Lombard, for their professionalism and their enthusiasm. Don't change a thing!
Stéphane, for his involvement with the historical file.
And of course, my associate since the beginning, Ronan. Always in the shadows, always ready to dispel my doubts.
VINCENT

My deep thanks to Gauthier and Vincent for their trust, their enthusiasm, and their commitment to this project. Thank you to the team at Le Lombard: Florence, Eric, Rebekah, Charlotte, Clémentine, Diane, and especially Camille, for her dedication, her rigour and how well and closely she worked with us.
Thank you to Dominique Demanet and Commandant Lejeune for the military resources.
Thank you to Elvire for her talent and her patience.
Thank you to the pope, Charles Michel, and Barack Obama for their support and unswerving friendship.
Finally, thank you to my father for his help, as indispensable as ever.
THOMAS

The historical file at the end of this book was created in partnership with Stéphane Dubreil, journalist at *Guerres & Histoire*.

Art director:
Eric Laurin

Book design:
Rebekah Paulovich

A big thank you to my Kiwi friend Dan Withers, 2nd Battalion, Parachute Regiment, for his help with many details of military life and parlance.
JEROME

'In September of 1940, the Italian army invades Egypt from Libya. Mussolini expects a triumph against a hard-pressed British Army. Yet, in four short months, the Italians suffer complete disaster, and the British even march into Libya! Everything changes with the arrival of Rommel and the Afrika Korps in February 1941, though. The initiative shifts back to the Axis, and as early as April 1941, the Desert Fox threatens Egypt. The situation is dire, but a time of peril is also a time for courage ...'

Original title: The Regiment – L'histoire vraie du SAS / livre 1
Original edition: © Éditions du Lombard (Dargaud-Lombard s.a.) 2017, by Legrain, Brugeas
www.lelombard.com
All rights reserved
English translation: © 2018 Cinebook Ltd
Translator: Jerome Saincantin
Editor: Erica Olson Jeffrey
Lettering and text layout: Design Amorandi
Printed in Spain by EGEDSA
This edition first published in Great Britain in 2019 by
Cinebook Ltd
56 Beech Avenue
Canterbury, Kent
CT4 7TA
www.cinebook.com
A CIP catalogue record for this book is available from the British Library
ISBN 978-1-84918-446-5

9th CINEBOOK
The 9th Art Publisher

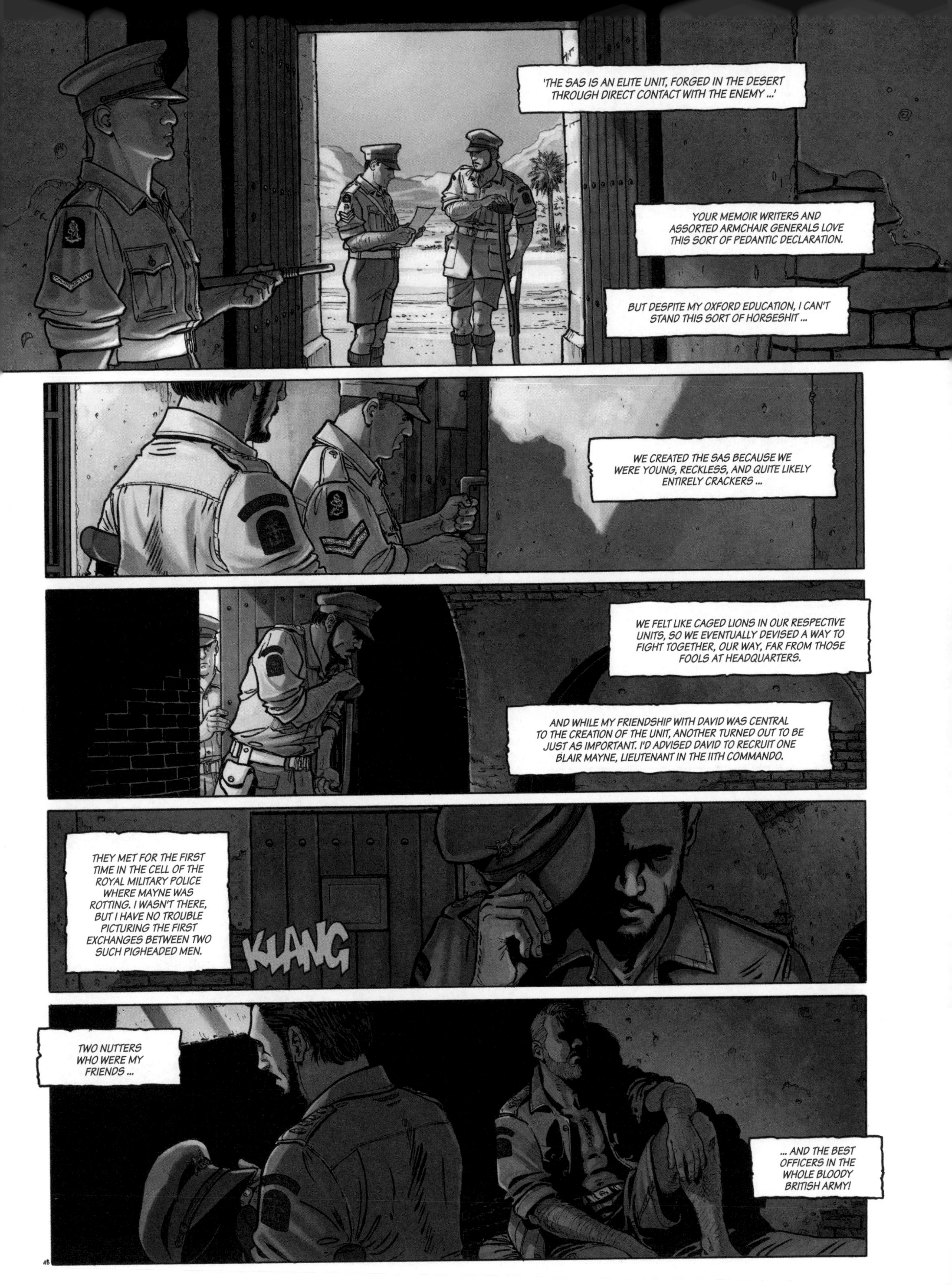
'THE SAS IS AN ELITE UNIT, FORGED IN THE DESERT THROUGH DIRECT CONTACT WITH THE ENEMY ...'
YOUR MEMOIR WRITERS AND ASSORTED ARMCHAIR GENERALS LOVE THIS SORT OF PEDANTIC DECLARATION.
BUT DESPITE MY OXFORD EDUCATION, I CAN'T STAND THIS SORT OF HORSESHIT ...
WE CREATED THE SAS BECAUSE WE WERE YOUNG, RECKLESS, AND QUITE LIKELY ENTIRELY CRACKERS ...
WE FELT LIKE CAGED LIONS IN OUR RESPECTIVE UNITS, SO WE EVENTUALLY DEVISED A WAY TO FIGHT TOGETHER, OUR WAY, FAR FROM THOSE FOOLS AT HEADQUARTERS.
AND WHILE MY FRIENDSHIP WITH DAVID WAS CENTRAL TO THE CREATION OF THE UNIT, ANOTHER TURNED OUT TO BE JUST AS IMPORTANT. I'D ADVISED DAVID TO RECRUIT ONE BLAIR MAYNE, LIEUTENANT IN THE 11TH COMMANDO.
THEY MET FOR THE FIRST TIME IN THE CELL OF THE ROYAL MILITARY POLICE WHERE MAYNE WAS ROTTING. I WASN'T THERE, BUT I HAVE NO TROUBLE PICTURING THE FIRST EXCHANGES BETWEEN TWO SUCH PIGHEADED MEN.
KLANG
TWO NUTTERS WHO WERE MY FRIENDS ...
... AND THE BEST OFFICERS IN THE WHOLE BLOODY BRITISH ARMY!

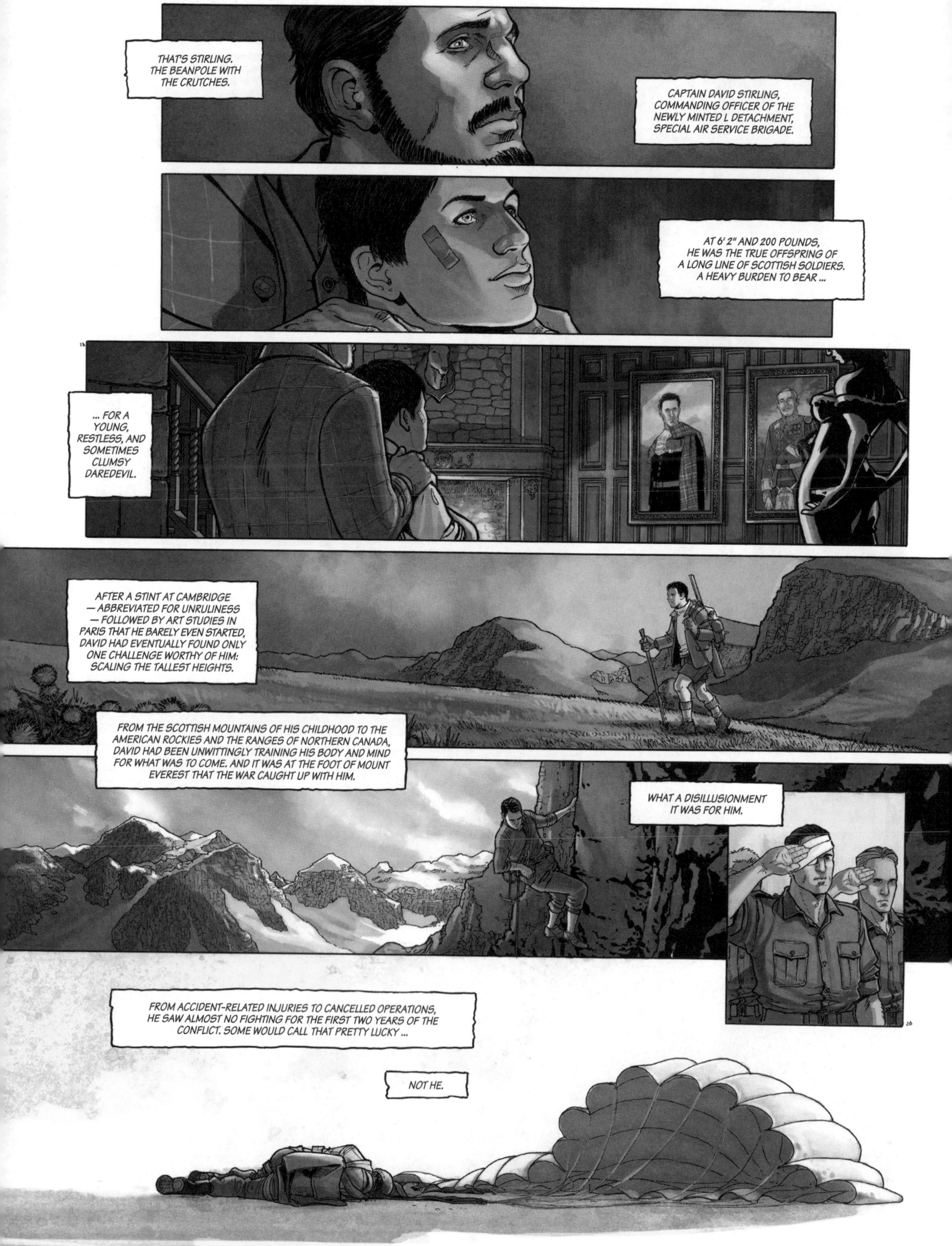
THAT'S STIRLING. THE BEANPOLE WITH THE CRUTCHES.
CAPTAIN DAVID STIRLING, COMMANDING OFFICER OF THE NEWLY MINTED L DETACHMENT, SPECIAL AIR SERVICE BRIGADE.
AT 6' 2" AND 200 POUNDS, HE WAS THE TRUE OFFSPRING OF A LONG LINE OF SCOTTISH SOLDIERS. A HEAVY BURDEN TO BEAR ...
... FOR A YOUNG, RESTLESS, AND SOMETIMES CLUMSY DAREDEVIL.
AFTER A STINT AT CAMBRIDGE — ABBREVIATED FOR UNRULINESS — FOLLOWED BY ART STUDIES IN PARIS THAT HE BARELY EVEN STARTED, DAVID HAD EVENTUALLY FOUND ONLY ONE CHALLENGE WORTHY OF HIM: SCALING THE TALLEST HEIGHTS.
FROM THE SCOTTISH MOUNTAINS OF HIS CHILDHOOD TO THE AMERICAN ROCKIES AND THE RANGES OF NORTHERN CANADA, DAVID HAD BEEN UNWITTINGLY TRAINING HIS BODY AND MIND FOR WHAT WAS TO COME. AND IT WAS AT THE FOOT OF MOUNT EVEREST THAT THE WAR CAUGHT UP WITH HIM.
WHAT A DISILLUSIONMENT IT WAS FOR HIM.
FROM ACCIDENT-RELATED INJURIES TO CANCELLED OPERATIONS, HE SAW ALMOST NO FIGHTING FOR THE FIRST TWO YEARS OF THE CONFLICT. SOME WOULD CALL THAT PRETTY LUCKY ...
NOT HE.

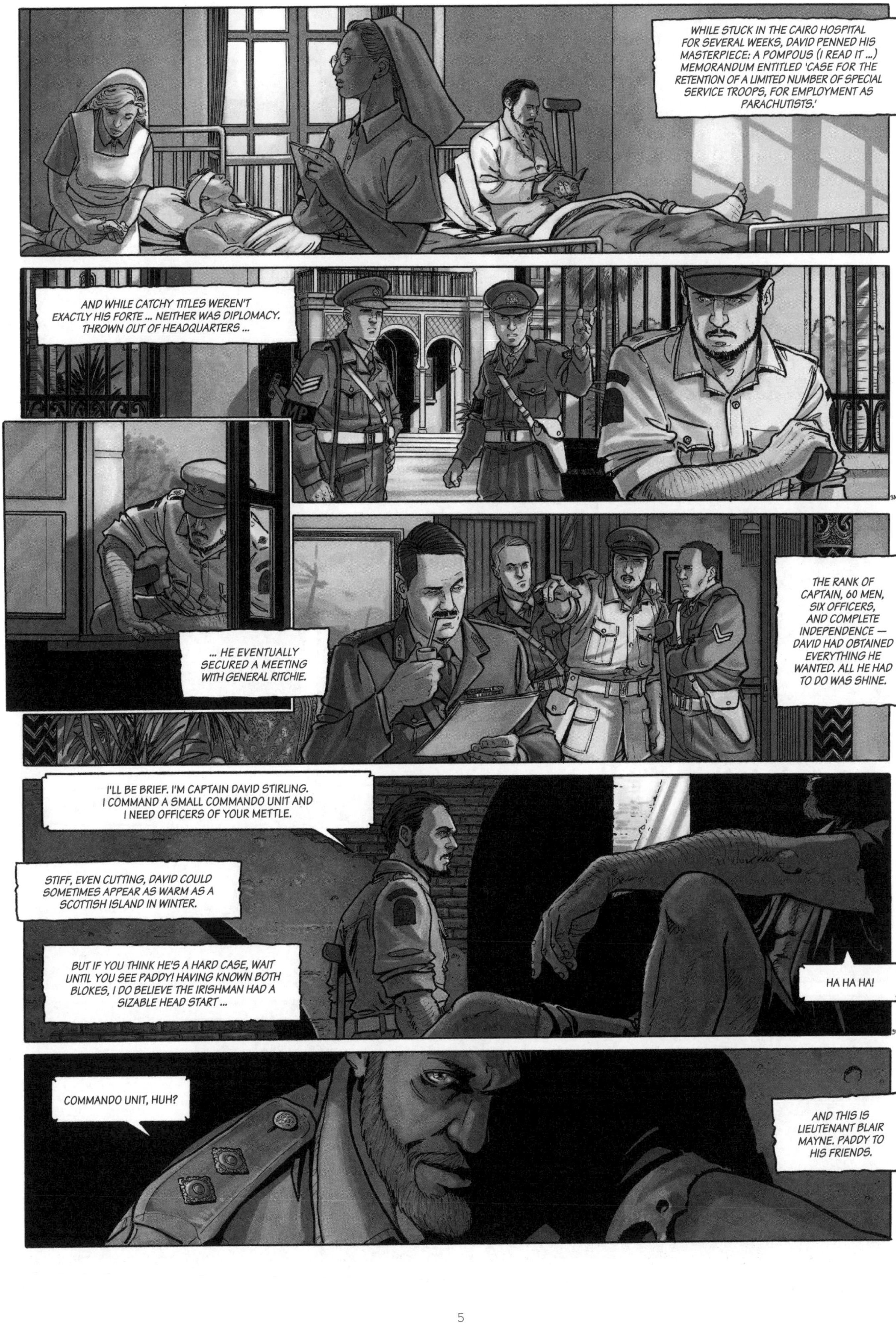
WHILE STUCK IN THE CAIRO HOSPITAL FOR SEVERAL WEEKS, DAVID PENNED HIS MASTERPIECE: A POMPOUS (I READ IT ...) MEMORANDUM ENTITLED 'CASE FOR THE RETENTION OF A LIMITED NUMBER OF SPECIAL SERVICE TROOPS, FOR EMPLOYMENT AS PARACHUTISTS.'
AND WHILE CATCHY TITLES WEREN'T EXACTLY HIS FORTE ... NEITHER WAS DIPLOMACY. THROWN OUT OF HEADQUARTERS ...
MP
... HE EVENTUALLY SECURED A MEETING WITH GENERAL RITCHIE.
THE RANK OF CAPTAIN, 60 MEN, SIX OFFICERS, AND COMPLETE INDEPENDENCE — DAVID HAD OBTAINED EVERYTHING HE WANTED. ALL HE HAD TO DO WAS SHINE.
I'LL BE BRIEF. I'M CAPTAIN DAVID STIRLING. I COMMAND A SMALL COMMANDO UNIT AND I NEED OFFICERS OF YOUR METTLE.
STIFF, EVEN CUTTING, DAVID COULD SOMETIMES APPEAR AS WARM AS A SCOTTISH ISLAND IN WINTER.
BUT IF YOU THINK HE'S A HARD CASE, WAIT UNTIL YOU SEE PADDY! HAVING KNOWN BOTH BLOKES, I DO BELIEVE THE IRISHMAN HAD A SIZABLE HEAD START ...
HA HA HA!
COMMANDO UNIT, HUH?
AND THIS IS LIEUTENANT BLAIR MAYNE. PADDY TO HIS FRIENDS.

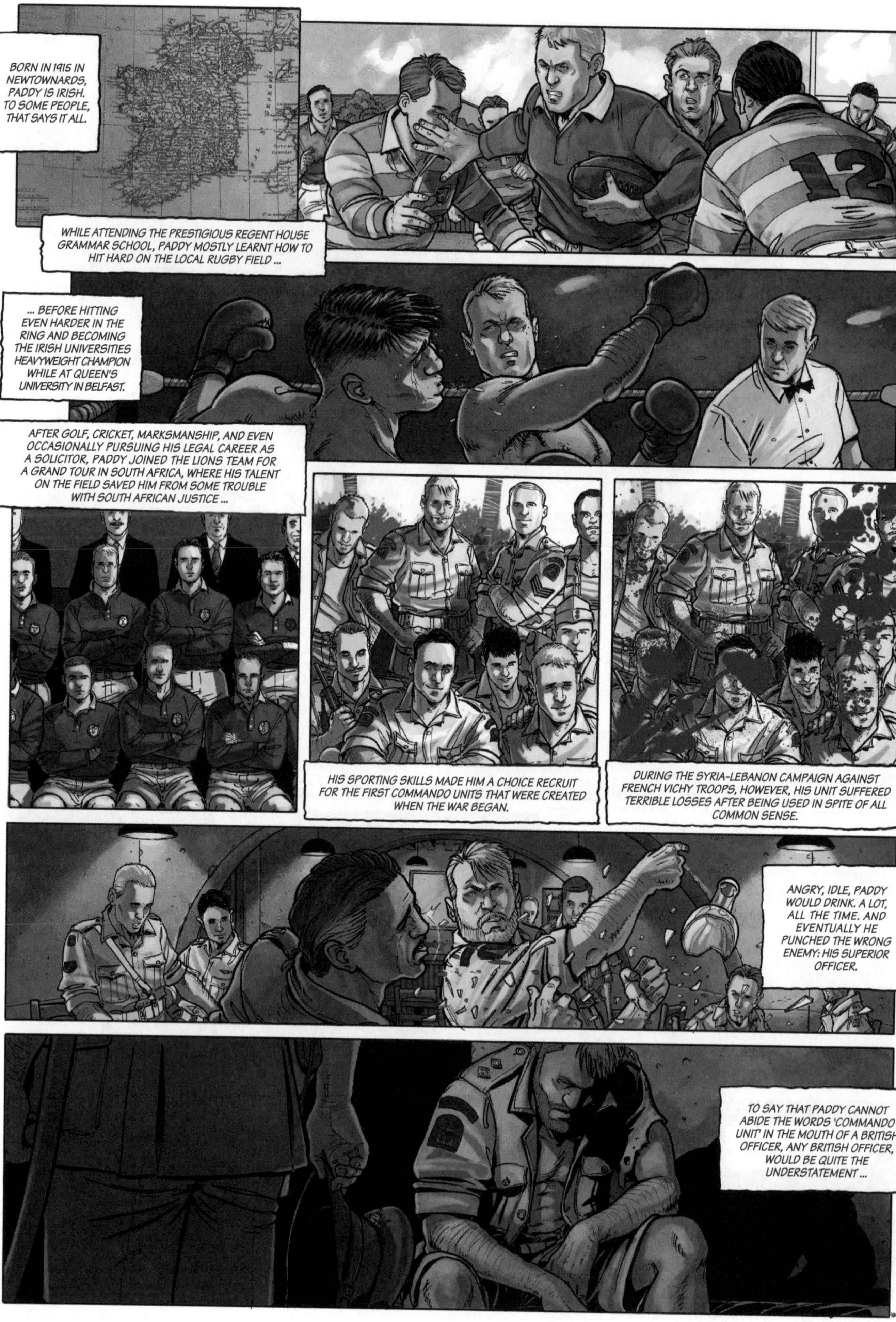
BORN IN 1915 IN NEWTOWNARDS, PADDY IS IRISH. TO SOME PEOPLE, THAT SAYS IT ALL.
WHILE ATTENDING THE PRESTIGIOUS REGENT HOUSE GRAMMAR SCHOOL, PADDY MOSTLY LEARNT HOW TO HIT HARD ON THE LOCAL RUGBY FIELD ...
... BEFORE HITTING EVEN HARDER IN THE RING AND BECOMING THE IRISH UNIVERSITIES HEAVYWEIGHT CHAMPION WHILE AT QUEEN'S UNIVERSITY IN BELFAST.
AFTER GOLF, CRICKET, MARKSMANSHIP, AND EVEN OCCASIONALLY PURSUING HIS LEGAL CAREER AS A SOLICITOR, PADDY JOINED THE LIONS TEAM FOR A GRAND TOUR IN SOUTH AFRICA, WHERE HIS TALENT ON THE FIELD SAVED HIM FROM SOME TROUBLE WITH SOUTH AFRICAN JUSTICE ...
HIS SPORTING SKILLS MADE HIM A CHOICE RECRUIT FOR THE FIRST COMMANDO UNITS THAT WERE CREATED WHEN THE WAR BEGAN.
DURING THE SYRIA-LEBANON CAMPAIGN AGAINST FRENCH VICHY TROOPS, HOWEVER, HIS UNIT SUFFERED TERRIBLE LOSSES AFTER BEING USED IN SPITE OF ALL COMMON SENSE.
ANGRY, IDLE, PADDY WOULD DRINK. A LOT, ALL THE TIME. AND EVENTUALLY HE PUNCHED THE WRONG ENEMY: HIS SUPERIOR OFFICER.
TO SAY THAT PADDY CANNOT ABIDE THE WORDS 'COMMANDO UNIT' IN THE MOUTH OF A BRITISH OFFICER, ANY BRITISH OFFICER, WOULD BE QUITE THE UNDERSTATEMENT ...
12

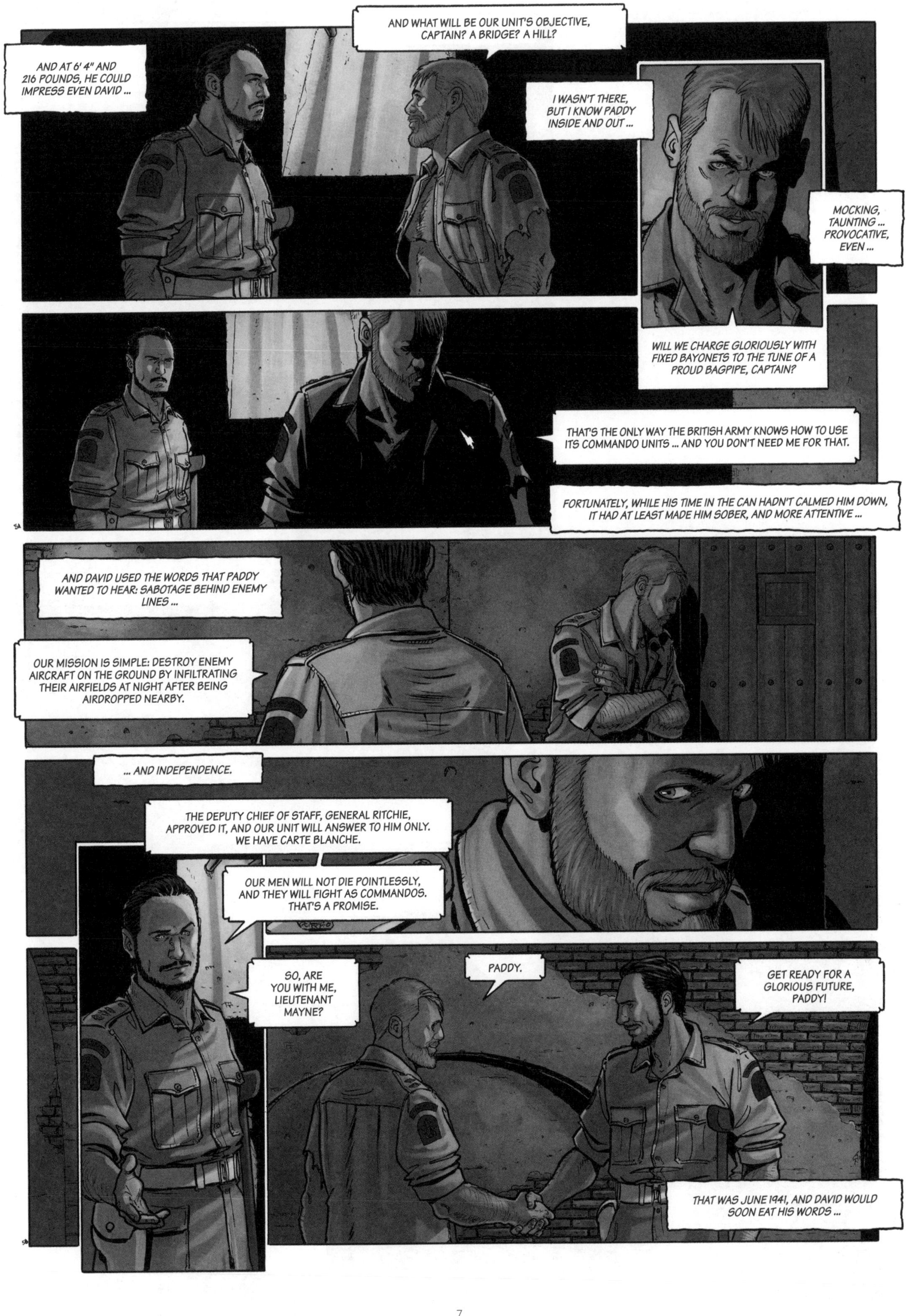
AND AT 6' 4" AND 216 POUNDS, HE COULD IMPRESS EVEN DAVID ...
AND WHAT WILL BE OUR UNIT'S OBJECTIVE, CAPTAIN? A BRIDGE? A HILL?
I WASN'T THERE, BUT I KNOW PADDY INSIDE AND OUT ...
MOCKING, TAUNTING ... PROVOCATIVE, EVEN ...
WILL WE CHARGE GLORIOUSLY WITH FIXED BAYONETS TO THE TUNE OF A PROUD BAGPIPE, CAPTAIN?
THAT'S THE ONLY WAY THE BRITISH ARMY KNOWS HOW TO USE ITS COMMANDO UNITS ... AND YOU DON'T NEED ME FOR THAT.
FORTUNATELY, WHILE HIS TIME IN THE CAN HADN'T CALMED HIM DOWN, IT HAD AT LEAST MADE HIM SOBER, AND MORE ATTENTIVE ...
AND DAVID USED THE WORDS THAT PADDY WANTED TO HEAR: SABOTAGE BEHIND ENEMY LINES ...
OUR MISSION IS SIMPLE: DESTROY ENEMY AIRCRAFT ON THE GROUND BY INFILTRATING THEIR AIRFIELDS AT NIGHT AFTER BEING AIRDROPPED NEARBY.
... AND INDEPENDENCE.
THE DEPUTY CHIEF OF STAFF, GENERAL RITCHIE, APPROVED IT, AND OUR UNIT WILL ANSWER TO HIM ONLY. WE HAVE CARTE BLANCHE.
OUR MEN WILL NOT DIE POINTLESSLY, AND THEY WILL FIGHT AS COMMANDOS. THAT'S A PROMISE.
SO, ARE YOU WITH ME, LIEUTENANT MAYNE?
PADDY.
GET READY FOR A GLORIOUS FUTURE, PADDY!
THAT WAS JUNE 1941, AND DAVID WOULD SOON EAT HIS WORDS ...

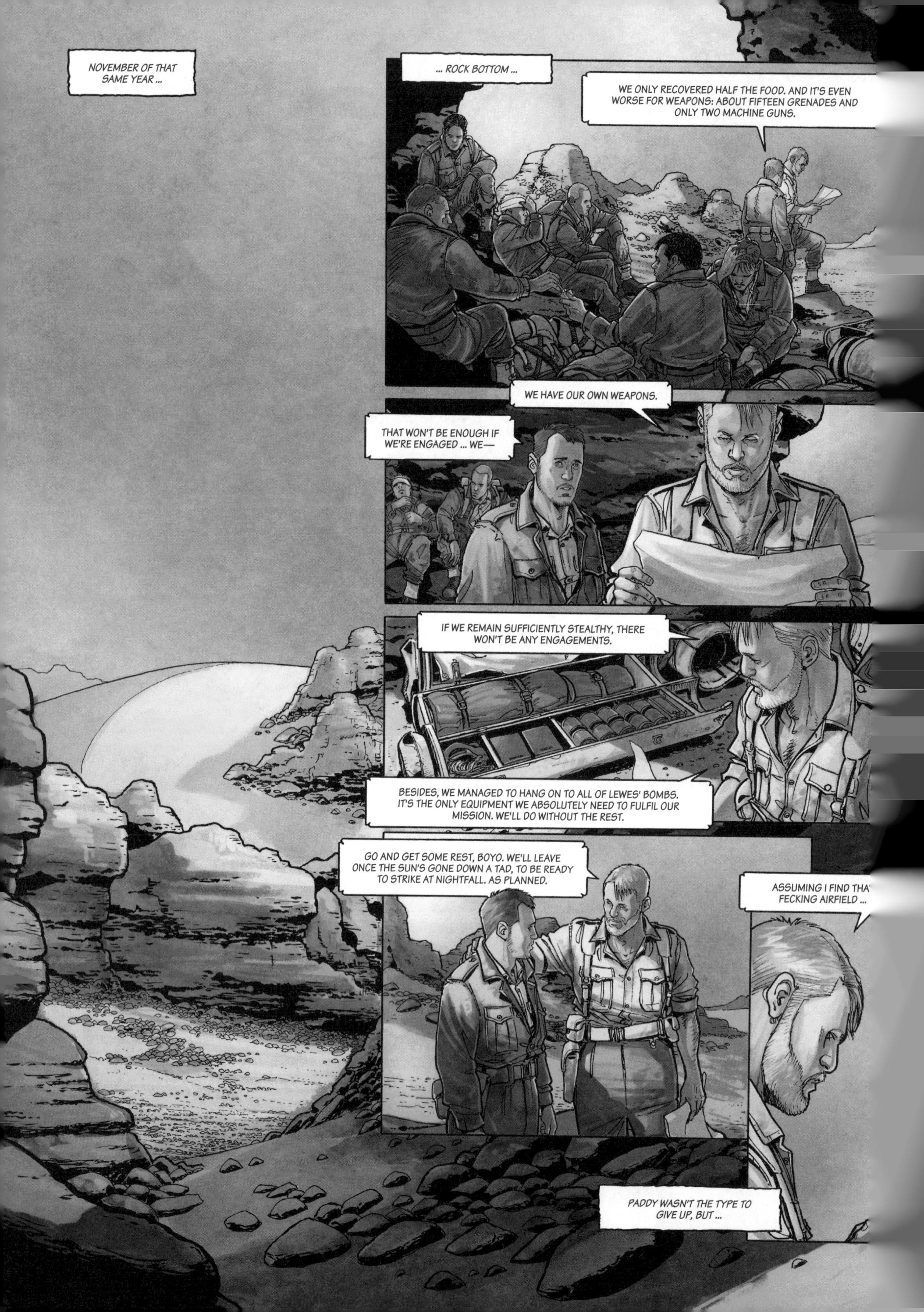

NOVEMBER OF THAT SAME YEAR ...
... ROCK BOTTOM ...
WE ONLY RECOVERED HALF THE FOOD. AND IT'S EVEN WORSE FOR WEAPONS: ABOUT FIFTEEN GRENADES AND ONLY TWO MACHINE GUNS.
WE HAVE OUR OWN WEAPONS.
THAT WON'T BE ENOUGH IF WE'RE ENGAGED ... WE—
IF WE REMAIN SUFFICIENTLY STEALTHY, THERE WON'T BE ANY ENGAGEMENTS.
BESIDES, WE MANAGED TO HANG ON TO ALL OF LEWES' BOMBS. IT'S THE ONLY EQUIPMENT WE ABSOLUTELY NEED TO FULFIL OUR MISSION. WE'LL DO WITHOUT THE REST.
GO AND GET SOME REST, BOYO. WE'LL LEAVE ONCE THE SUN'S GONE DOWN A TAD, TO BE READY TO STRIKE AT NIGHTFALL. AS PLANNED.
ASSUMING I FIND THAT FECKING AIRFIELD ...
PADDY WASN'T THE TYPE TO GIVE UP, BUT ...

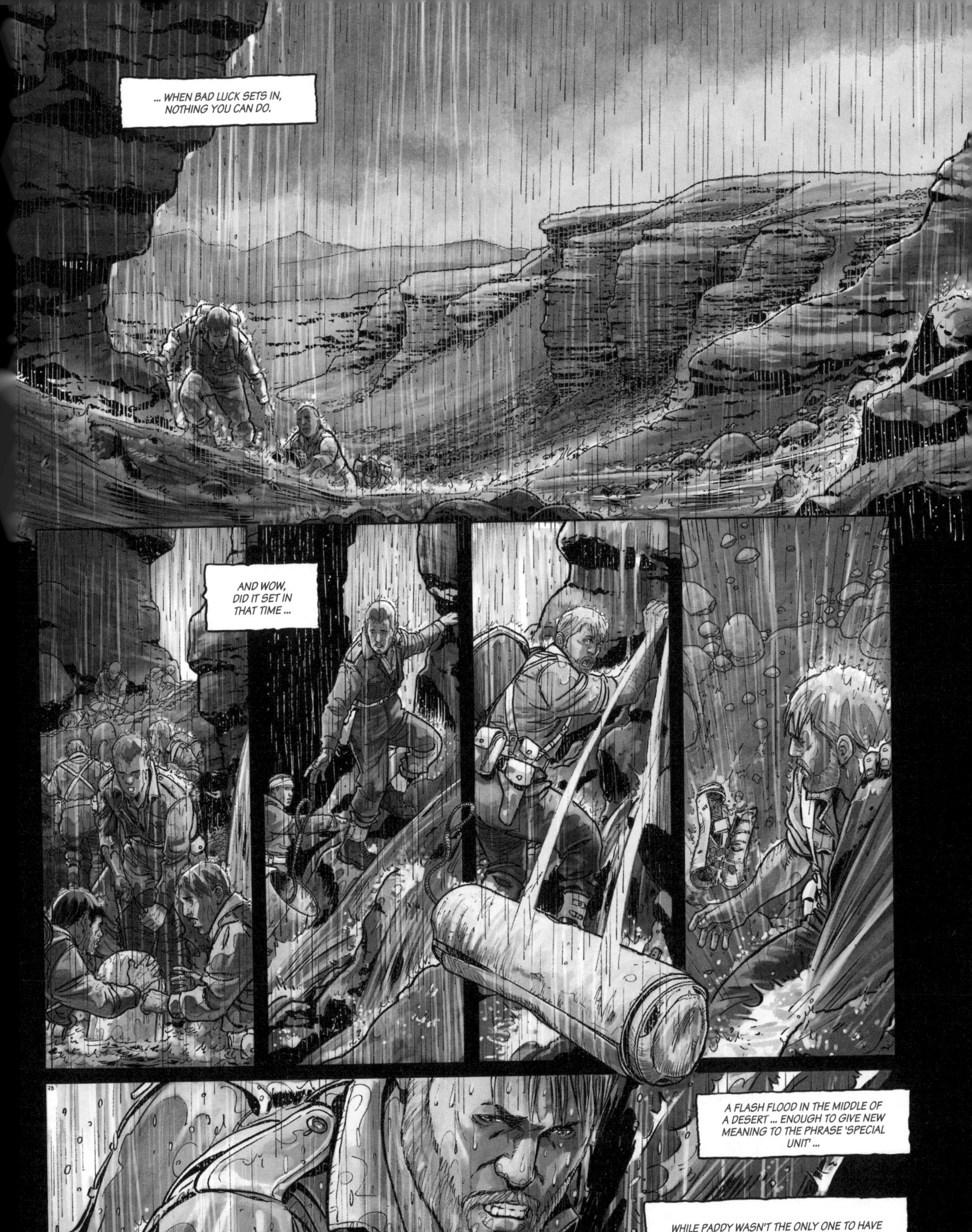
... WHEN BAD LUCK SETS IN,
NOTHING YOU CAN DO.
AND WOW,
DID IT SET IN
THAT TIME ...
A FLASH FLOOD IN THE MIDDLE OF A DESERT ... ENOUGH TO GIVE NEW MEANING TO THE PHRASE 'SPECIAL UNIT' ...
WHILE PADDY WASN'T THE ONLY ONE TO HAVE ROTTEN LUCK DURING THAT OPERATION ...

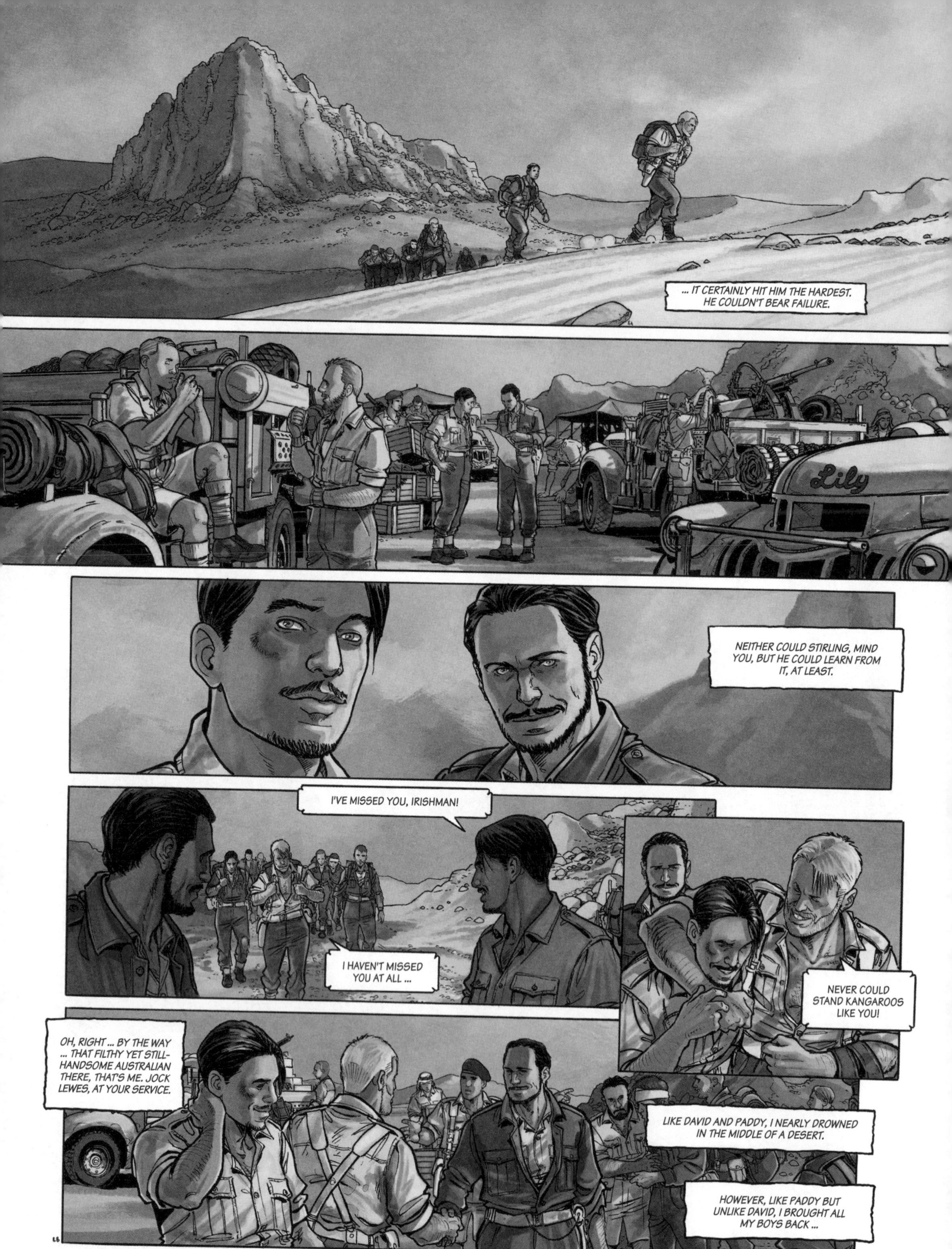
... IT CERTAINLY HIT HIM THE HARDEST. HE COULDN'T BEAR FAILURE.
NEITHER COULD STIRLING, MIND YOU, BUT HE COULD LEARN FROM IT, AT LEAST.
I'VE MISSED YOU, IRISHMAN!
I HAVEN'T MISSED YOU AT ALL ...
NEVER COULD STAND KANGAROOS LIKE YOU!
OH, RIGHT ... BY THE WAY ... THAT FILTHY YET STILL-HANDSOME AUSTRALIAN THERE, THAT'S ME. JOCK LEWES, AT YOUR SERVICE.
LIKE DAVID AND PADDY, I NEARLY DROWNED IN THE MIDDLE OF A DESERT.
HOWEVER, LIKE PADDY BUT UNLIKE DAVID, I BROUGHT ALL MY BOYS BACK ...

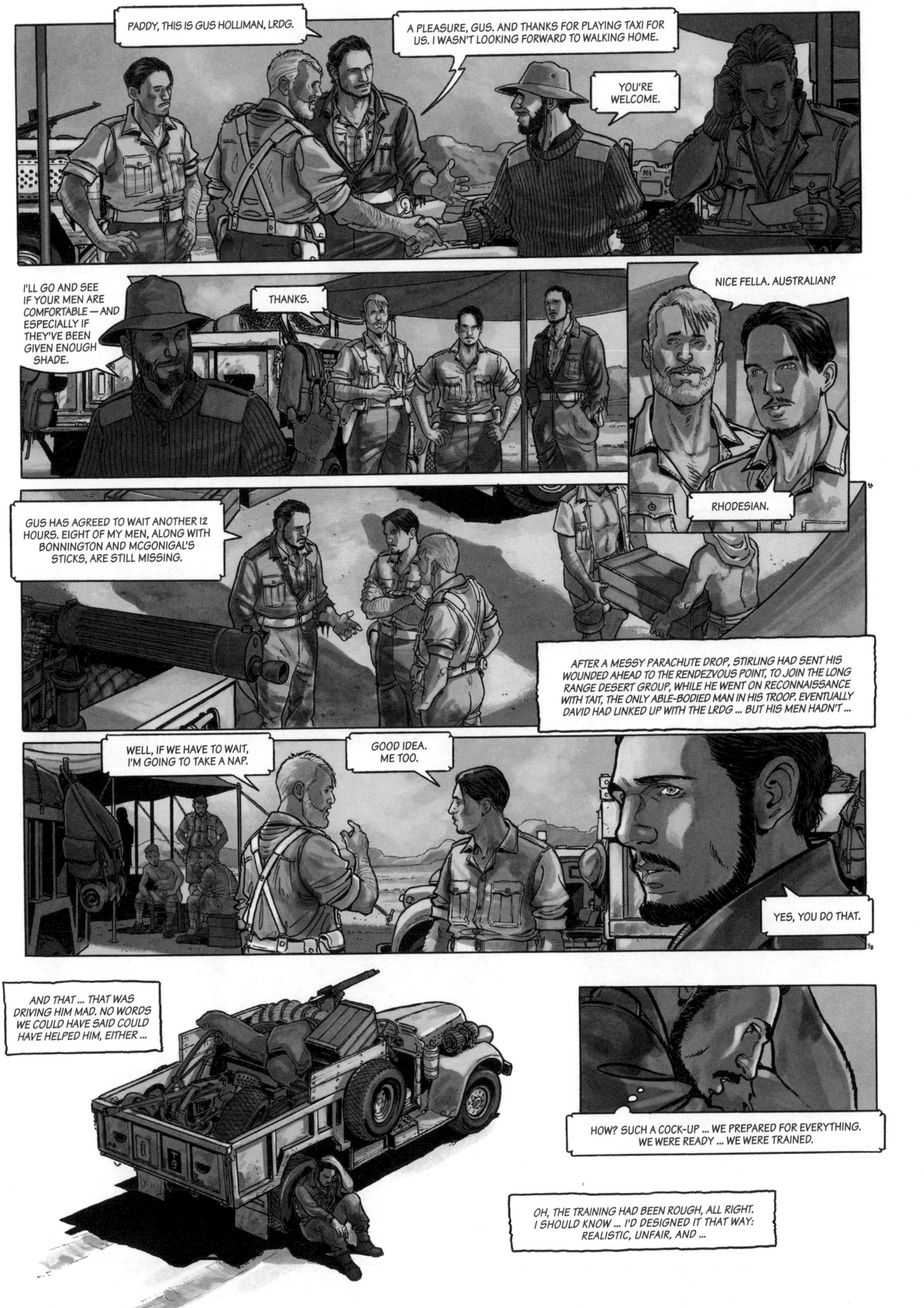
PADDY, THIS IS GUS HOLLIMAN, LRDG.
A PLEASURE, GUS. AND THANKS FOR PLAYING TAXI FOR US. I WASN'T LOOKING FORWARD TO WALKING HOME.
YOU'RE WELCOME.
I'LL GO AND SEE IF YOUR MEN ARE COMFORTABLE — AND ESPECIALLY IF THEY'VE BEEN GIVEN ENOUGH SHADE.
THANKS.
NICE FELLA. AUSTRALIAN?
RHODESIAN.
GUS HAS AGREED TO WAIT ANOTHER 12 HOURS. EIGHT OF MY MEN, ALONG WITH BONNINGTON AND MCGONIGAL'S STICKS, ARE STILL MISSING.
AFTER A MESSY PARACHUTE DROP, STIRLING HAD SENT HIS WOUNDED AHEAD TO THE RENDEZVOUS POINT, TO JOIN THE LONG RANGE DESERT GROUP, WHILE HE WENT ON RECONNAISSANCE WITH TAIT, THE ONLY ABLE-BODIED MAN IN HIS TROOP. EVENTUALLY DAVID HAD LINKED UP WITH THE LRDG ... BUT HIS MEN HADN'T ...
WELL, IF WE HAVE TO WAIT, I'M GOING TO TAKE A NAP.
GOOD IDEA. ME TOO.
YES, YOU DO THAT.
AND THAT ... THAT WAS DRIVING HIM MAD. NO WORDS WE COULD HAVE SAID COULD HAVE HELPED HIM, EITHER ...
HOW? SUCH A COCK-UP ... WE PREPARED FOR EVERYTHING. WE WERE READY ... WE WERE TRAINED.
OH, THE TRAINING HAD BEEN ROUGH, ALL RIGHT. I SHOULD KNOW ... I'D DESIGNED IT THAT WAY: REALISTIC, UNFAIR, AND ...

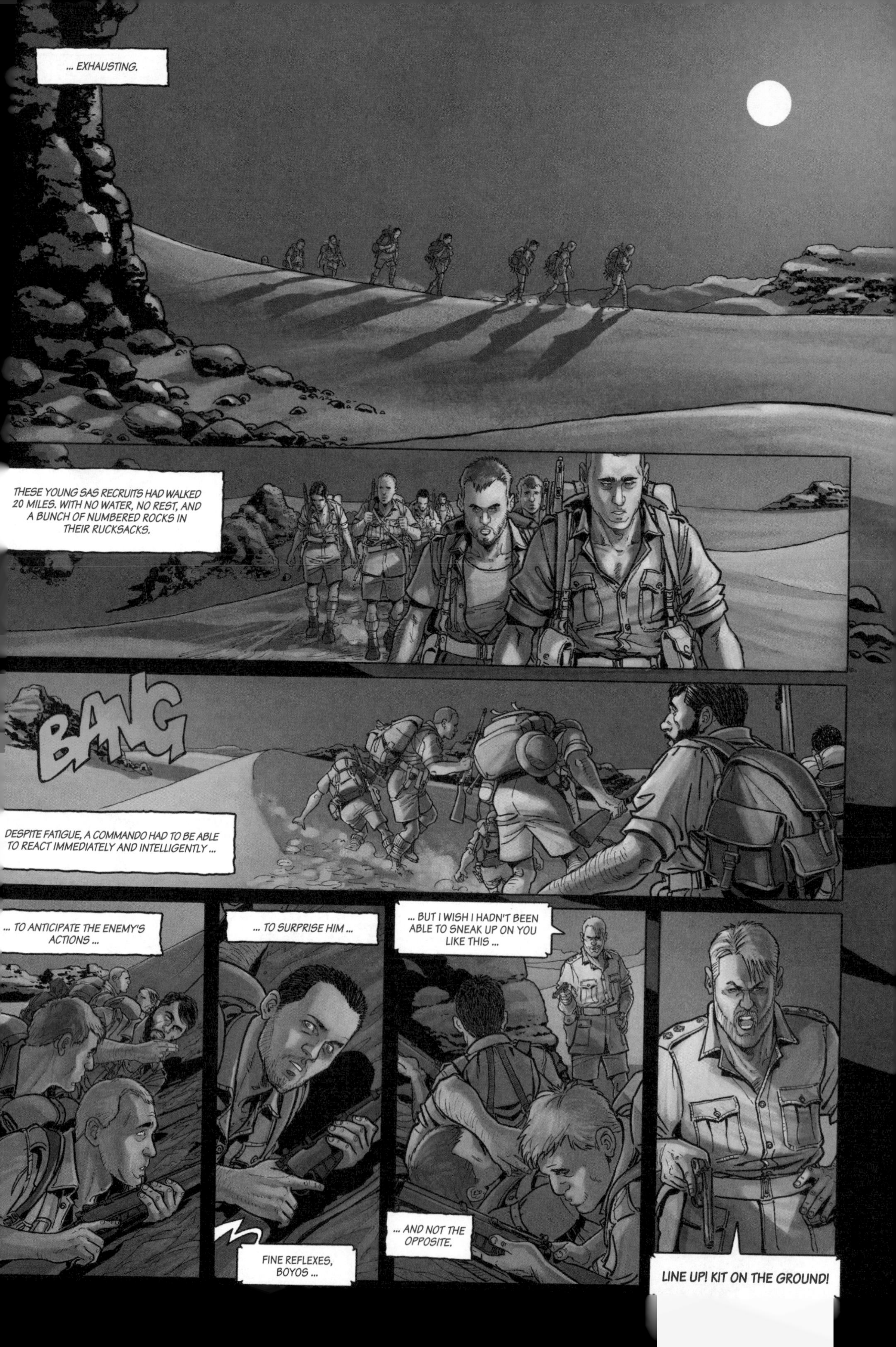
... EXHAUSTING.
THESE YOUNG SAS RECRUITS HAD WALKED 20 MILES. WITH NO WATER, NO REST, AND A BUNCH OF NUMBERED ROCKS IN THEIR RUCKSACKS.
BANG
DESPITE FATIGUE, A COMMANDO HAD TO BE ABLE TO REACT IMMEDIATELY AND INTELLIGENTLY ...
... TO ANTICIPATE THE ENEMY'S ACTIONS ...
... TO SURPRISE HIM ...
FINE REFLEXES, BOYOS ...
... BUT I WISH I HADN'T BEEN ABLE TO SNEAK UP ON YOU LIKE THIS ...
... AND NOT THE OPPOSITE.
LINE UP! KIT ON THE GROUND!

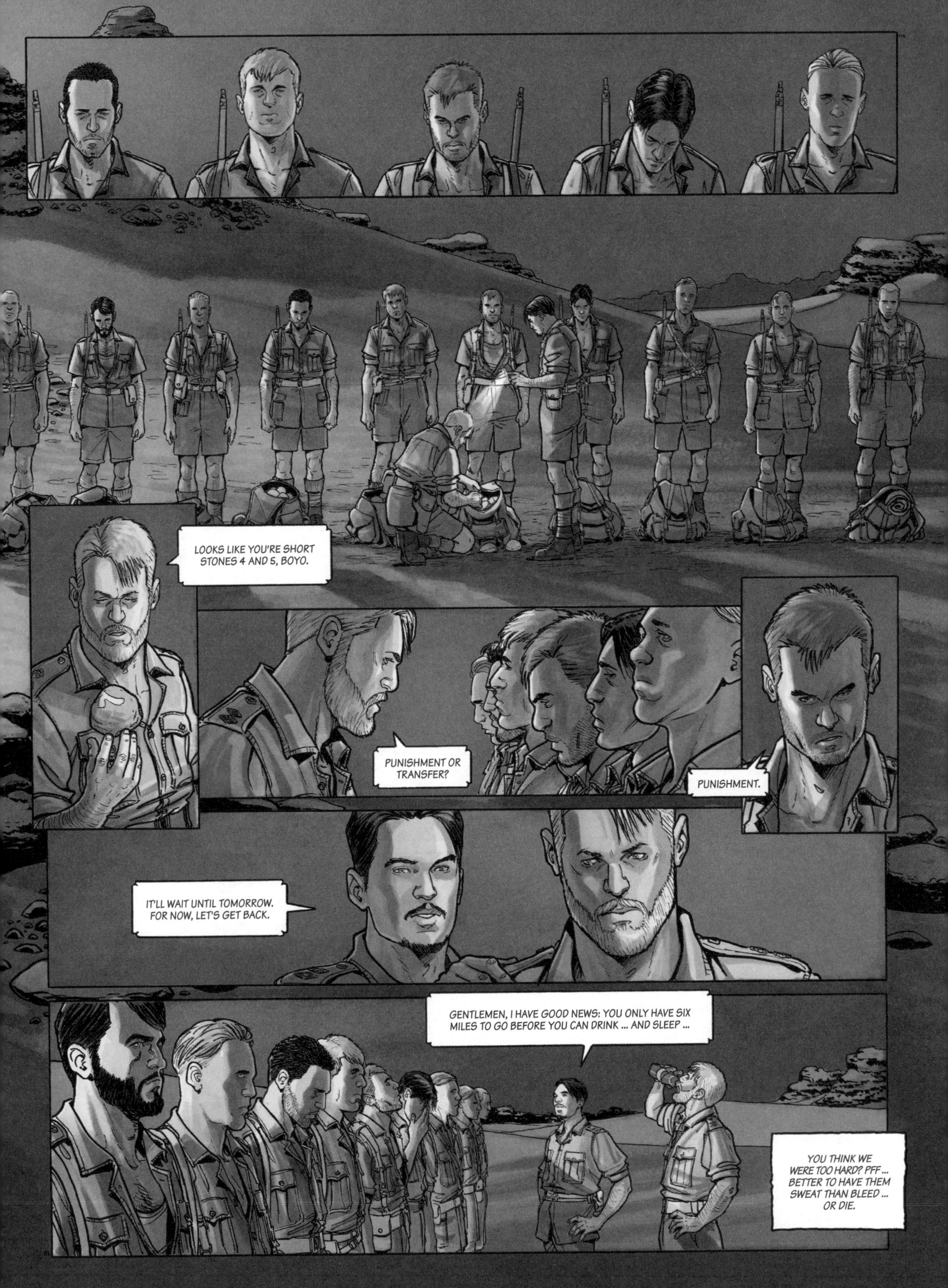
LOOKS LIKE YOU'RE SHORT STONES 4 AND 5, BOYO.
PUNISHMENT OR TRANSFER?
PUNISHMENT.
IT'LL WAIT UNTIL TOMORROW. FOR NOW, LET'S GET BACK.
GENTLEMEN, I HAVE GOOD NEWS: YOU ONLY HAVE SIX MILES TO GO BEFORE YOU CAN DRINK ... AND SLEEP ...
YOU THINK WE WERE TOO HARD? PFF ... BETTER TO HAVE THEM SWEAT THAN BLEED ... OR DIE.

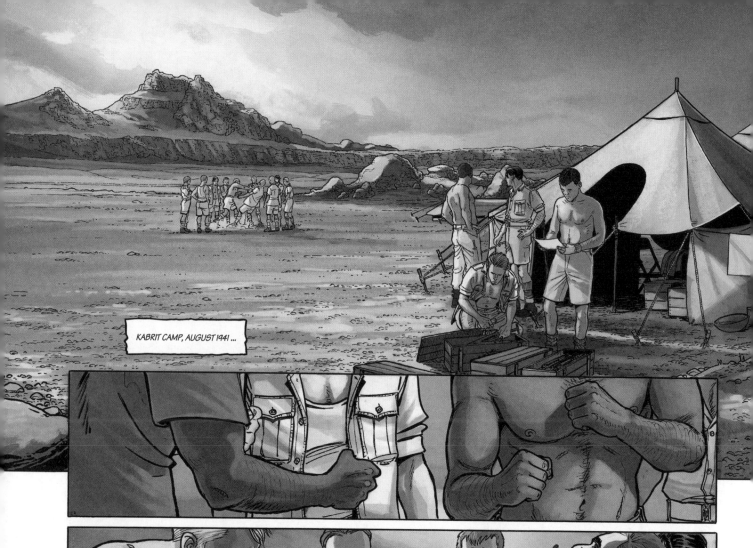

KABRIT CAMP, AUGUST 1941 ...

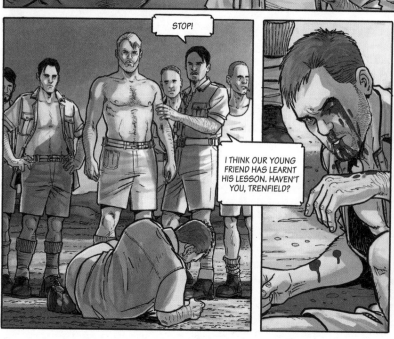

STOP!

I THINK OUR YOUNG FRIEND HAS LEARNT HIS LESSON. HAVEN'T YOU, TRENFIELD?

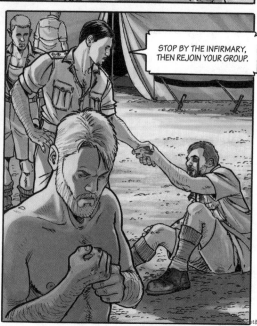

STOP BY THE INFIRMARY, THEN REJOIN YOUR GROUP.

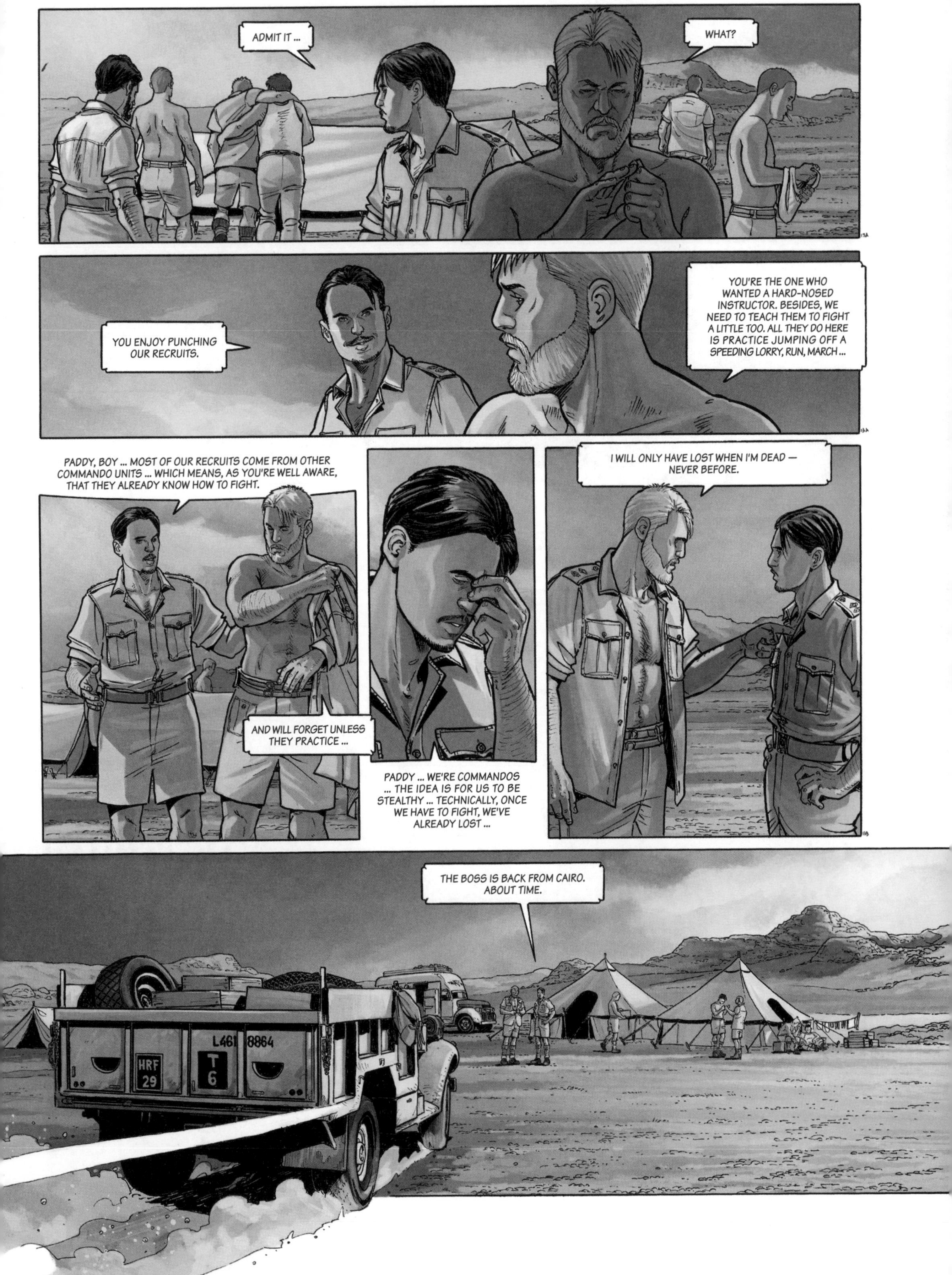
ADMIT IT ...
WHAT?
YOU ENJOY PUNCHING OUR RECRUITS.
YOU'RE THE ONE WHO WANTED A HARD-NOSED INSTRUCTOR. BESIDES, WE NEED TO TEACH THEM TO FIGHT A LITTLE TOO. ALL THEY DO HERE IS PRACTICE JUMPING OFF A SPEEDING LORRY, RUN, MARCH ...
PADDY, BOY ... MOST OF OUR RECRUITS COME FROM OTHER COMMANDO UNITS ... WHICH MEANS, AS YOU'RE WELL AWARE, THAT THEY ALREADY KNOW HOW TO FIGHT.
AND WILL FORGET UNLESS THEY PRACTICE ...
PADDY ... WE'RE COMMANDOS ... THE IDEA IS FOR US TO BE STEALTHY ... TECHNICALLY, ONCE WE HAVE TO FIGHT, WE'VE ALREADY LOST ...
I WILL ONLY HAVE LOST WHEN I'M DEAD — NEVER BEFORE.
THE BOSS IS BACK FROM CAIRO. ABOUT TIME.
L461 8864
HRF 29
T 6

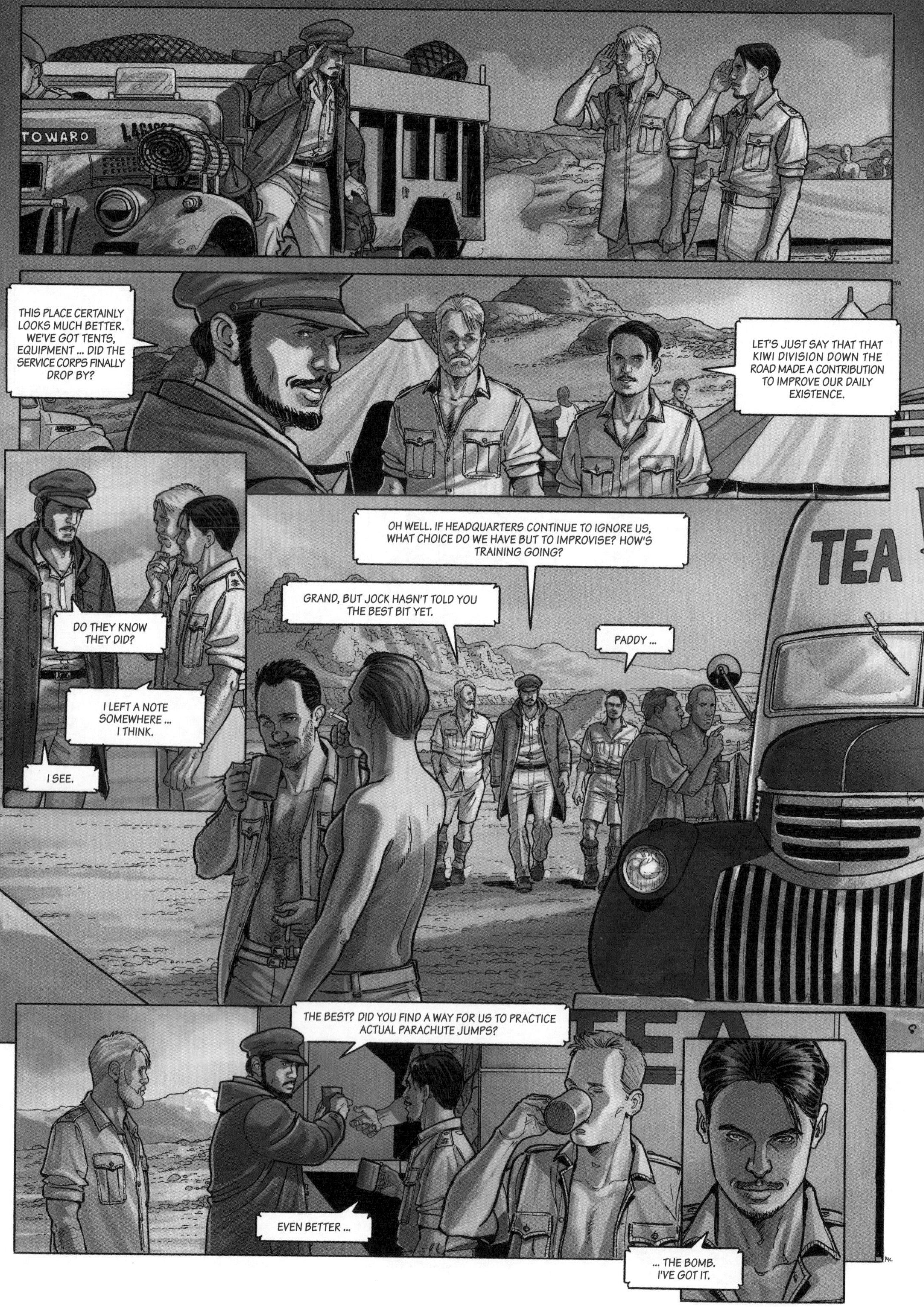

THIS PLACE CERTAINLY LOOKS MUCH BETTER. WE'VE GOT TENTS, EQUIPMENT ... DID THE SERVICE CORPS FINALLY DROP BY?
LET'S JUST SAY THAT THAT KIWI DIVISION DOWN THE ROAD MADE A CONTRIBUTION TO IMPROVE OUR DAILY EXISTENCE.
DO THEY KNOW THEY DID?
I LEFT A NOTE SOMEWHERE ... I THINK.
I SEE.
OH WELL. IF HEADQUARTERS CONTINUE TO IGNORE US, WHAT CHOICE DO WE HAVE BUT TO IMPROVISE? HOW'S TRAINING GOING?
GRAND, BUT JOCK HASN'T TOLD YOU THE BEST BIT YET.
PADDY ...
TEA
THE BEST? DID YOU FIND A WAY FOR US TO PRACTICE ACTUAL PARACHUTE JUMPS?
EVEN BETTER ...
... THE BOMB. I'VE GOT IT.

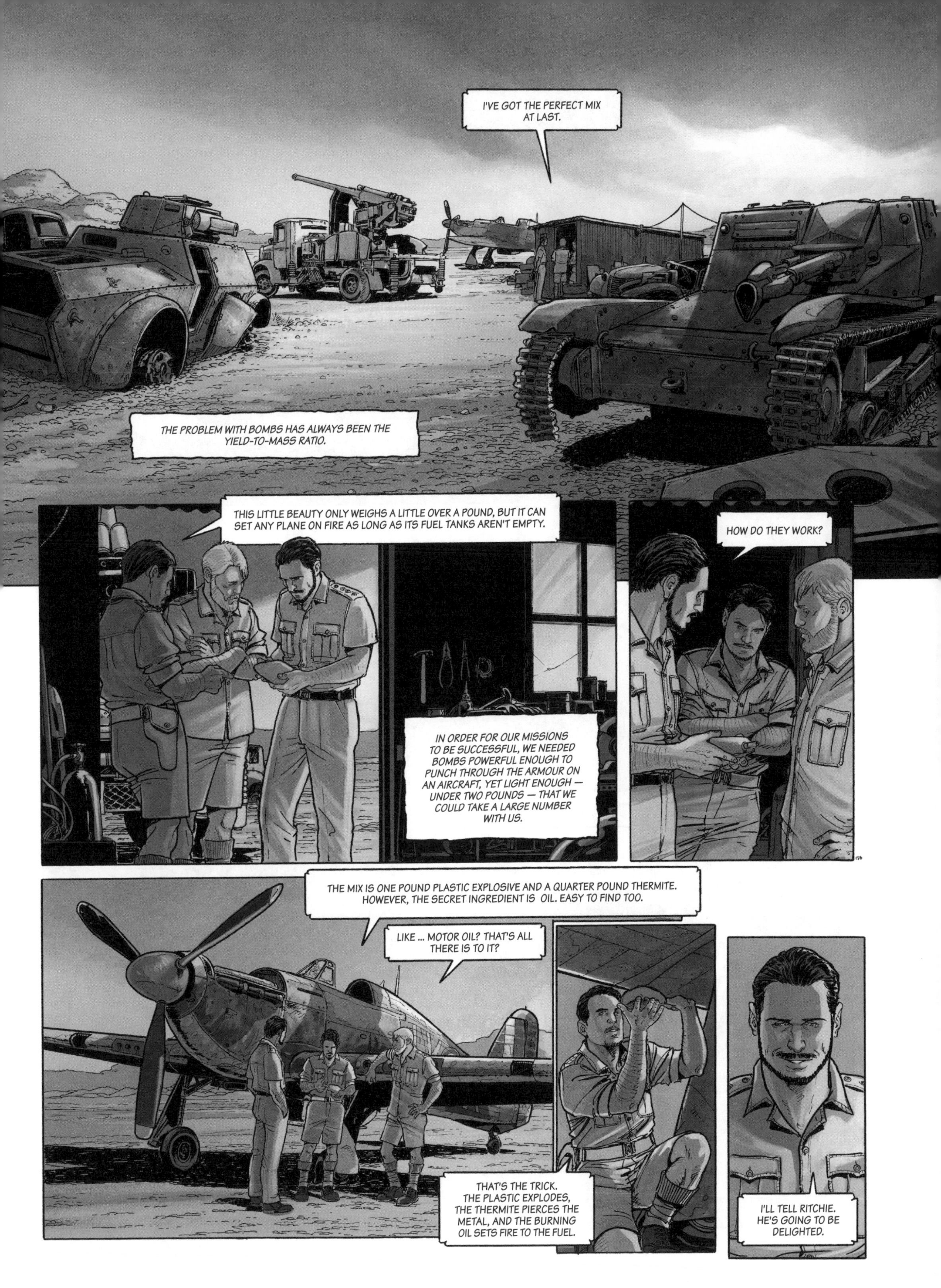
I'VE GOT THE PERFECT MIX AT LAST.
THE PROBLEM WITH BOMBS HAS ALWAYS BEEN THE YIELD-TO-MASS RATIO.
THIS LITTLE BEAUTY ONLY WEIGHS A LITTLE OVER A POUND, BUT IT CAN SET ANY PLANE ON FIRE AS LONG AS ITS FUEL TANKS AREN'T EMPTY.
IN ORDER FOR OUR MISSIONS TO BE SUCCESSFUL, WE NEEDED BOMBS POWERFUL ENOUGH TO PUNCH THROUGH THE ARMOUR ON AN AIRCRAFT, YET LIGHT ENOUGH — UNDER TWO POUNDS — THAT WE COULD TAKE A LARGE NUMBER WITH US.
HOW DO THEY WORK?
THE MIX IS ONE POUND PLASTIC EXPLOSIVE AND A QUARTER POUND THERMITE. HOWEVER, THE SECRET INGREDIENT IS OIL. EASY TO FIND TOO.
LIKE ... MOTOR OIL? THAT'S ALL THERE IS TO IT?
THAT'S THE TRICK. THE PLASTIC EXPLODES, THE THERMITE PIERCES THE METAL, AND THE BURNING OIL SETS FIRE TO THE FUEL.
I'LL TELL RITCHIE. HE'S GOING TO BE DELIGHTED.

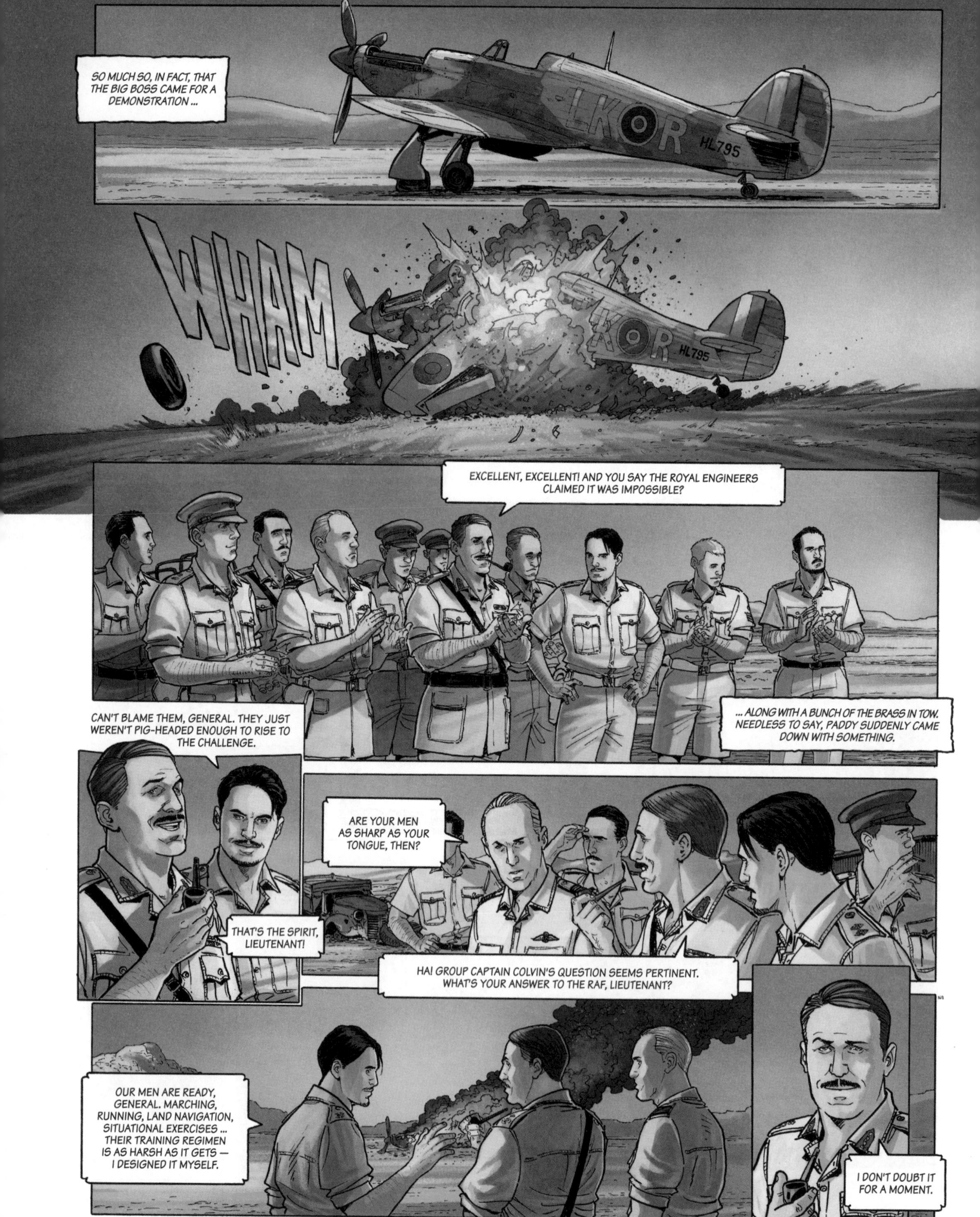
SO MUCH SO, IN FACT, THAT THE BIG BOSS CAME FOR A DEMONSTRATION ...
LK R
HL795
WHAM
K R
HL795
EXCELLENT, EXCELLENT! AND YOU SAY THE ROYAL ENGINEERS CLAIMED IT WAS IMPOSSIBLE?
... ALONG WITH A BUNCH OF THE BRASS IN TOW. NEEDLESS TO SAY, PADDY SUDDENLY CAME DOWN WITH SOMETHING.
CAN'T BLAME THEM, GENERAL. THEY JUST WEREN'T PIG-HEADED ENOUGH TO RISE TO THE CHALLENGE.
THAT'S THE SPIRIT, LIEUTENANT!
ARE YOUR MEN AS SHARP AS YOUR TONGUE, THEN?
HA! GROUP CAPTAIN COLVIN'S QUESTION SEEMS PERTINENT. WHAT'S YOUR ANSWER TO THE RAF, LIEUTENANT?
OUR MEN ARE READY, GENERAL. MARCHING, RUNNING, LAND NAVIGATION, SITUATIONAL EXERCISES ... THEIR TRAINING REGIMEN IS AS HARSH AS IT GETS — I DESIGNED IT MYSELF.
I DON'T DOUBT IT FOR A MOMENT.

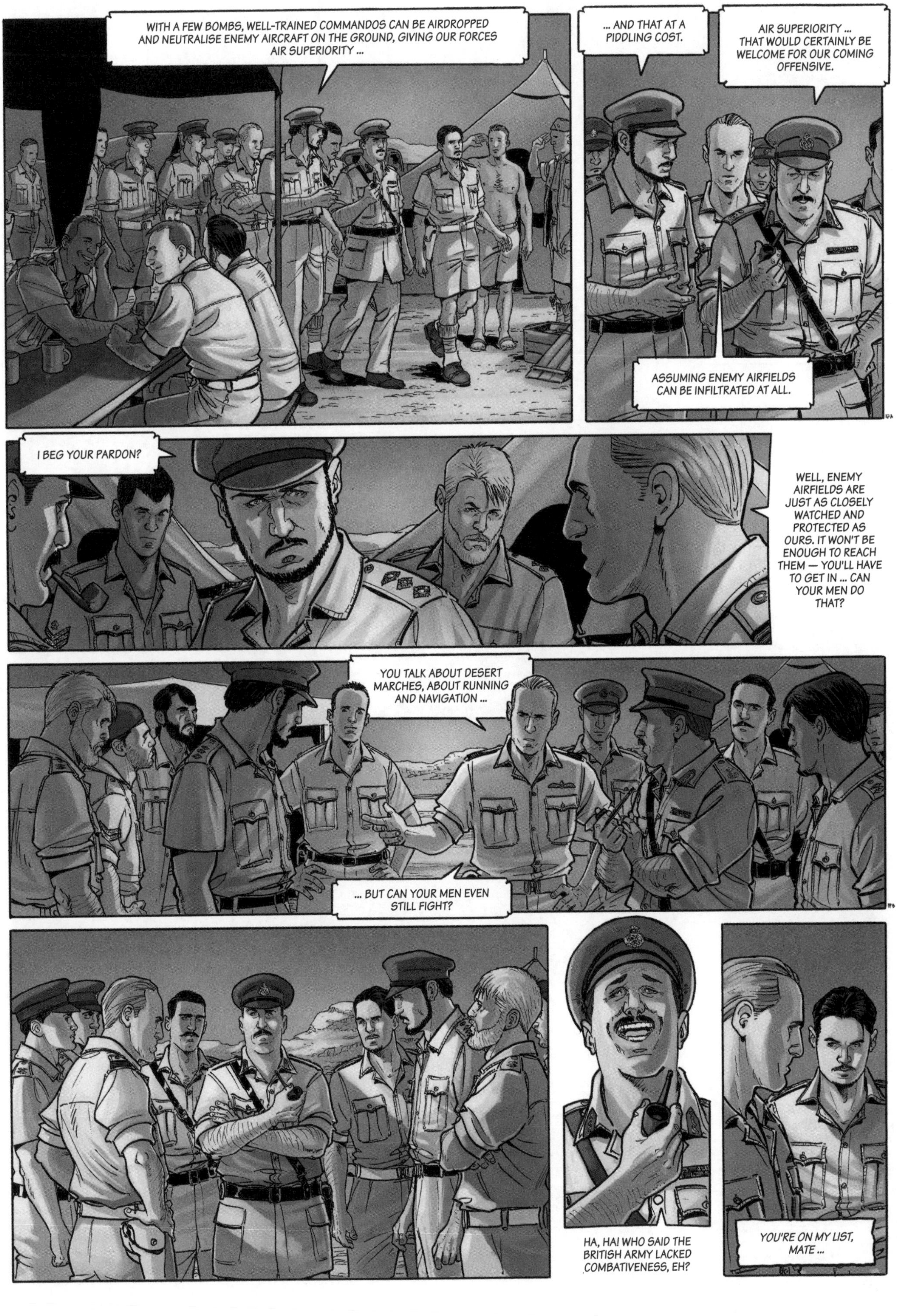

WITH A FEW BOMBS, WELL-TRAINED COMMANDOS CAN BE AIRDROPPED AND NEUTRALISE ENEMY AIRCRAFT ON THE GROUND, GIVING OUR FORCES AIR SUPERIORITY ...
... AND THAT AT A PIDDLING COST.
AIR SUPERIORITY ... THAT WOULD CERTAINLY BE WELCOME FOR OUR COMING OFFENSIVE.
ASSUMING ENEMY AIRFIELDS CAN BE INFILTRATED AT ALL.
I BEG YOUR PARDON?
WELL, ENEMY AIRFIELDS ARE JUST AS CLOSELY WATCHED AND PROTECTED AS OURS. IT WON'T BE ENOUGH TO REACH THEM — YOU'LL HAVE TO GET IN ... CAN YOUR MEN DO THAT?
YOU TALK ABOUT DESERT MARCHES, ABOUT RUNNING AND NAVIGATION ...
... BUT CAN YOUR MEN EVEN STILL FIGHT?
HA, HA! WHO SAID THE BRITISH ARMY LACKED COMBATIVENESS, EH?
YOU'RE ON MY LIST, MATE ...

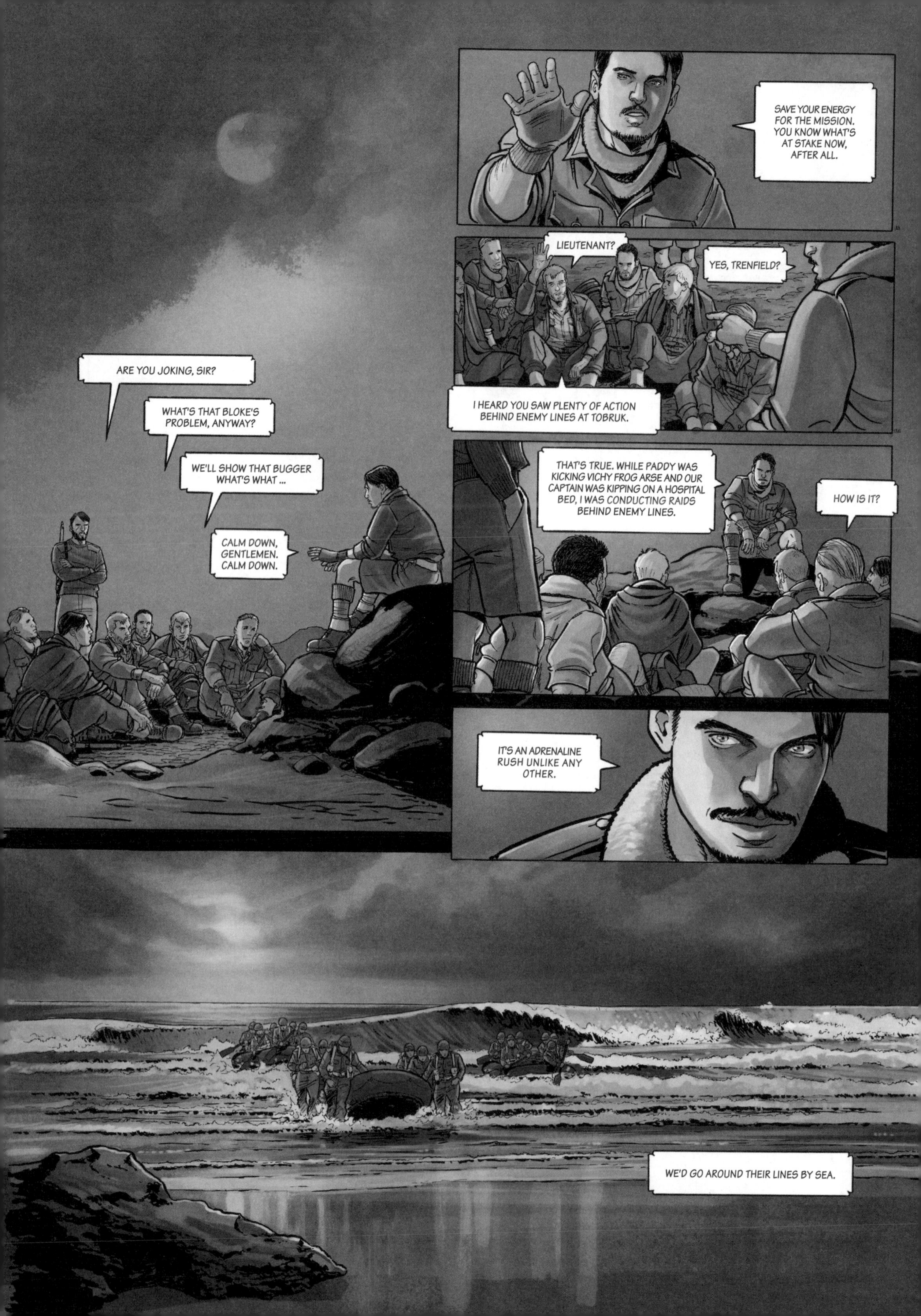

ARE YOU JOKING, SIR?
WHAT'S THAT BLOKE'S PROBLEM, ANYWAY?
WE'LL SHOW THAT BUGGER WHAT'S WHAT ...
CALM DOWN, GENTLEMEN. CALM DOWN.
SAVE YOUR ENERGY FOR THE MISSION. YOU KNOW WHAT'S AT STAKE NOW, AFTER ALL.
LIEUTENANT?
YES, TRENFIELD?
I HEARD YOU SAW PLENTY OF ACTION BEHIND ENEMY LINES AT TOBRUK.
THAT'S TRUE. WHILE PADDY WAS KICKING VICHY FROG ARSE AND OUR CAPTAIN WAS KIPPING ON A HOSPITAL BED, I WAS CONDUCTING RAIDS BEHIND ENEMY LINES.
HOW IS IT?
IT'S AN ADRENALINE RUSH UNLIKE ANY OTHER.
WE'D GO AROUND THEIR LINES BY SEA.

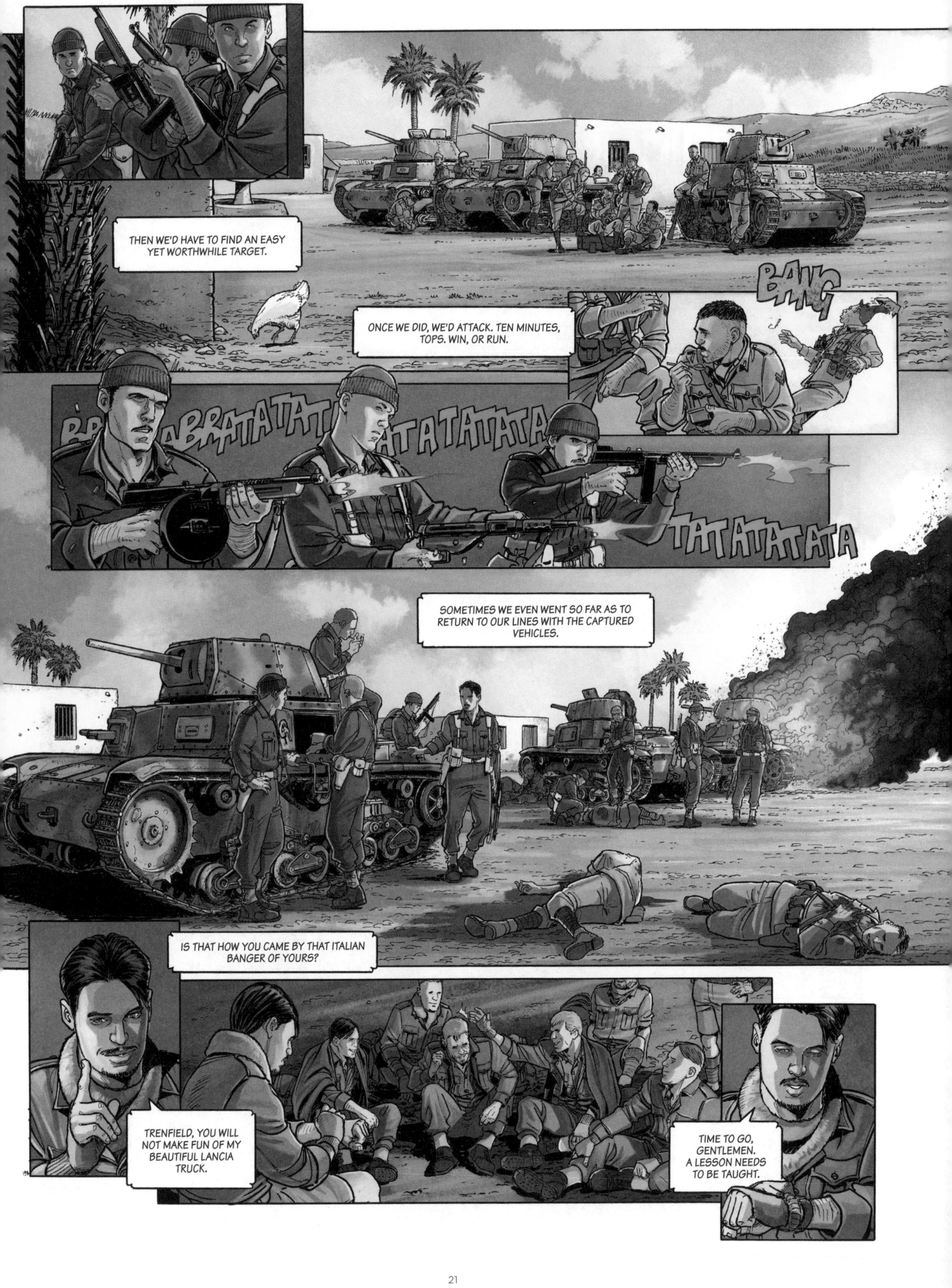
THEN WE'D HAVE TO FIND AN EASY YET WORTHWHILE TARGET.
ONCE WE DID, WE'D ATTACK. TEN MINUTES, TOPS. WIN, OR RUN.
BANG
BRATATATATATATATATATA
TATATATATATA
SOMETIMES WE EVEN WENT SO FAR AS TO RETURN TO OUR LINES WITH THE CAPTURED VEHICLES.
IS THAT HOW YOU CAME BY THAT ITALIAN BANGER OF YOURS?
TRENFIELD, YOU WILL NOT MAKE FUN OF MY BEAUTIFUL LANCIA TRUCK.
TIME TO GO, GENTLEMEN. A LESSON NEEDS TO BE TAUGHT.

HELIOPOLIS AIRFIELD, ON AN OCTOBER EVENING ...

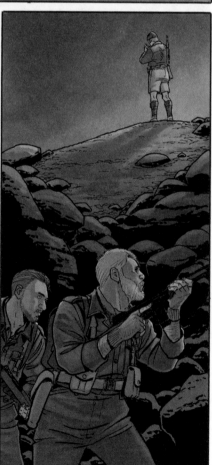

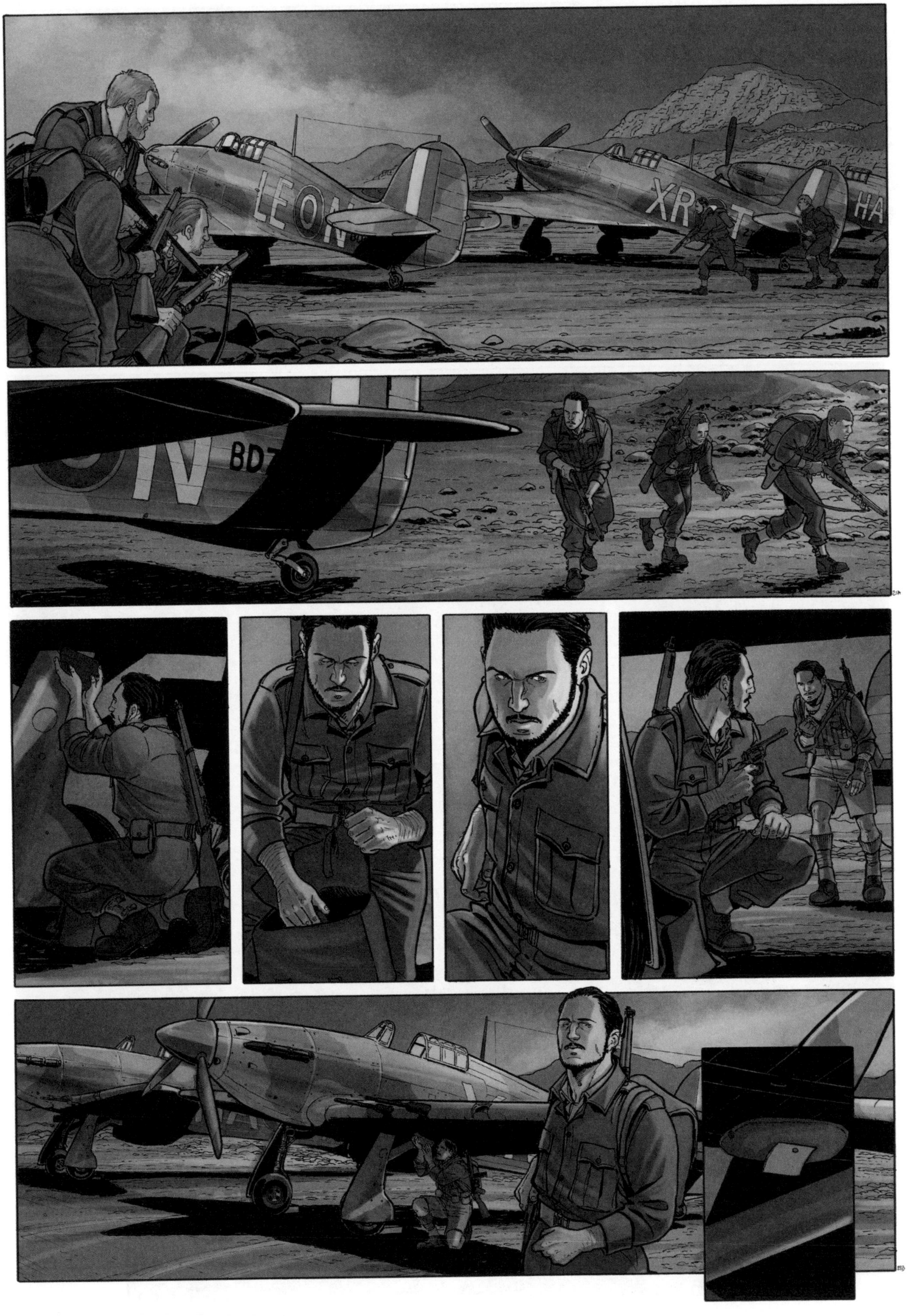

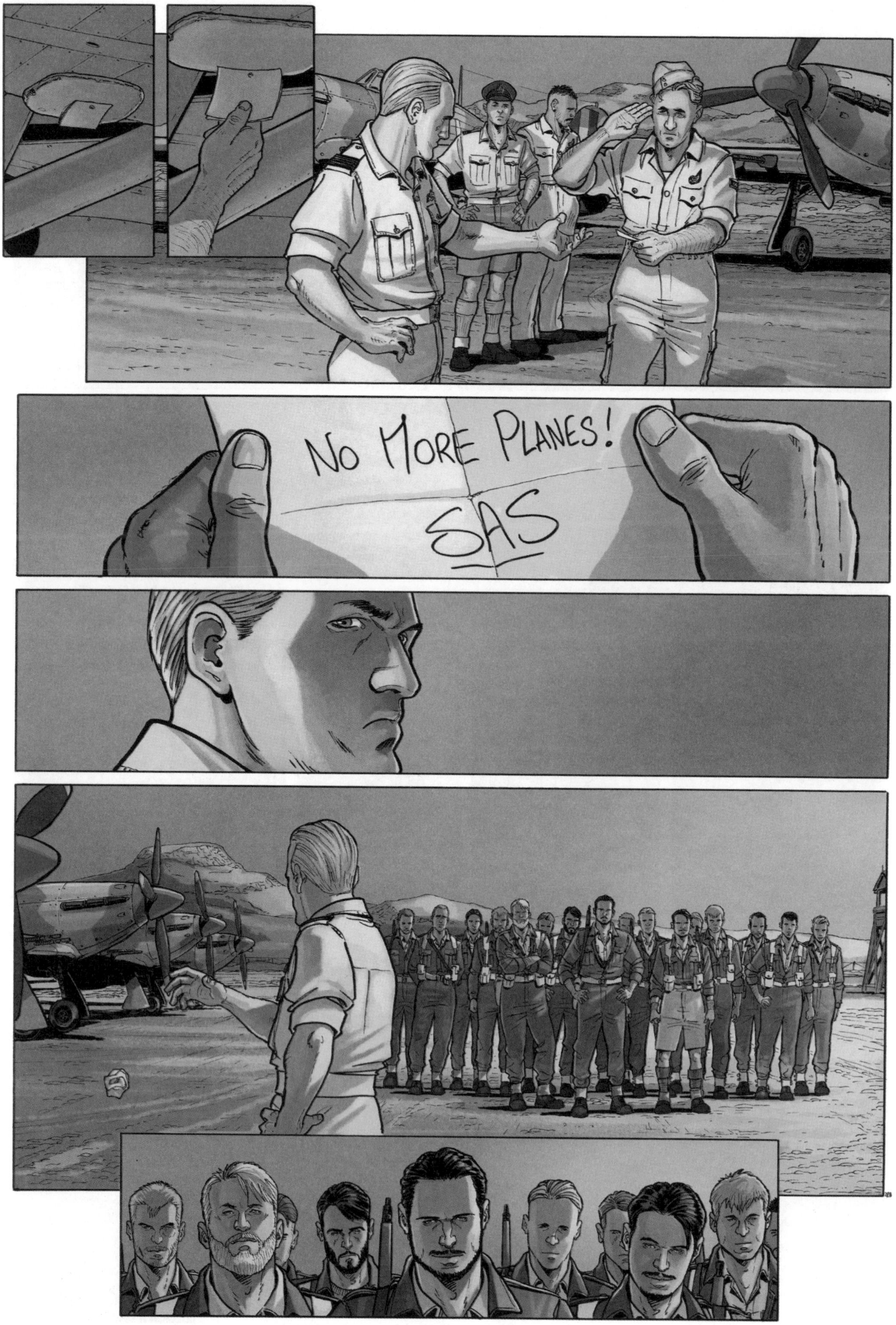
No More Planes!
SAS

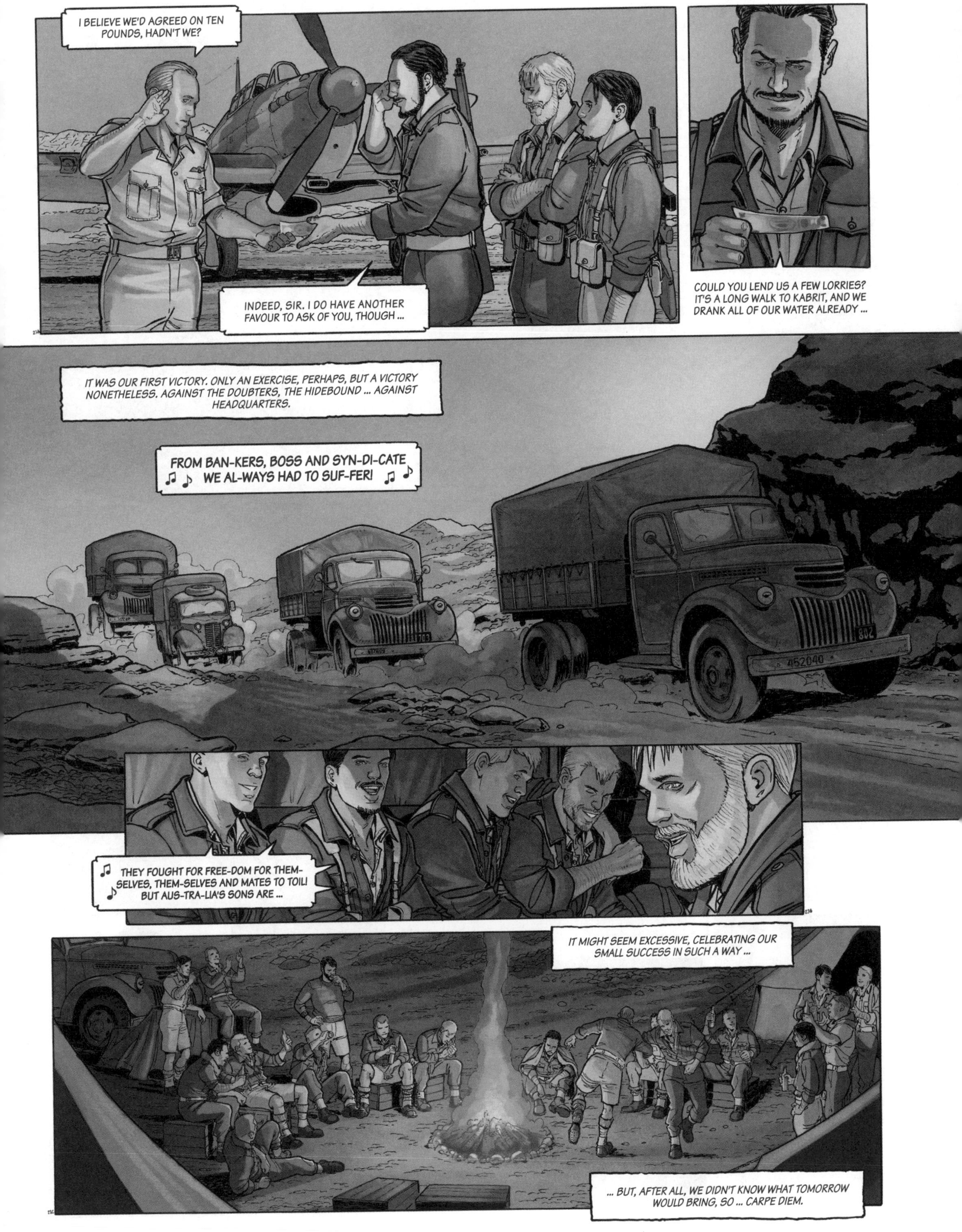
I BELIEVE WE'D AGREED ON TEN POUNDS, HADN'T WE?
INDEED, SIR. I DO HAVE ANOTHER FAVOUR TO ASK OF YOU, THOUGH ...
COULD YOU LEND US A FEW LORRIES? IT'S A LONG WALK TO KABRIT, AND WE DRANK ALL OF OUR WATER ALREADY ...
IT WAS OUR FIRST VICTORY. ONLY AN EXERCISE, PERHAPS, BUT A VICTORY NONETHELESS. AGAINST THE DOUBTERS, THE HIDEBOUND ... AGAINST HEADQUARTERS.
FROM BAN-KERS, BOSS AND SYN-DI-CATE ♫ ♪ WE AL-WAYS HAD TO SUF-FER! ♫ ♪
♫ THEY FOUGHT FOR FREE-DOM FOR THEM-SELVES, THEM-SELVES AND MATES TO TOIL! ♪ BUT AUS-TRA-LIA'S SONS ARE ...
IT MIGHT SEEM EXCESSIVE, CELEBRATING OUR SMALL SUCCESS IN SUCH A WAY ...
... BUT, AFTER ALL, WE DIDN'T KNOW WHAT TOMORROW WOULD BRING, SO ... CARPE DIEM.

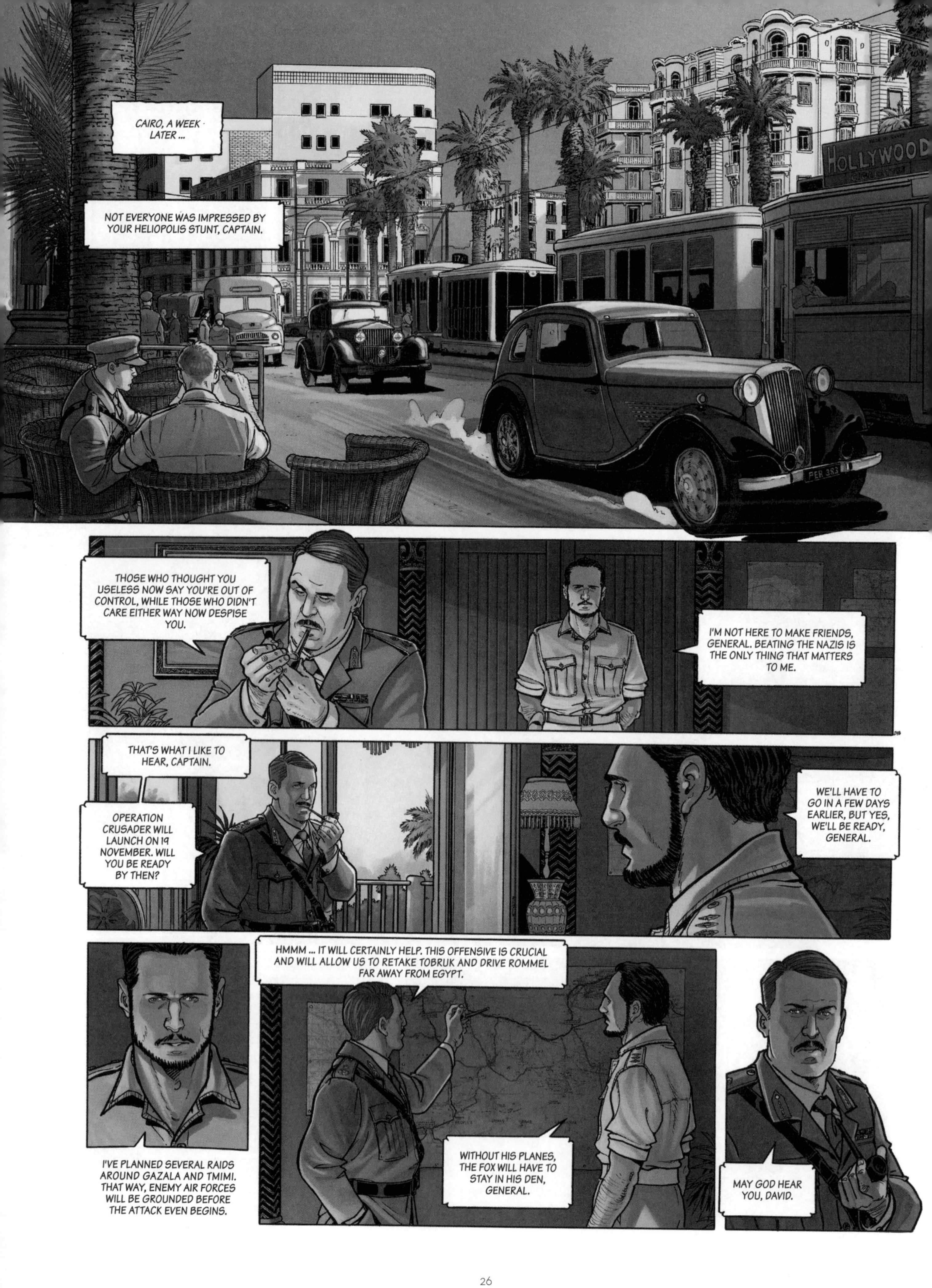

CAIRO, A WEEK LATER ...
HOLLYWOOD
NOT EVERYONE WAS IMPRESSED BY YOUR HELIOPOLIS STUNT, CAPTAIN.
THOSE WHO THOUGHT YOU USELESS NOW SAY YOU'RE OUT OF CONTROL, WHILE THOSE WHO DIDN'T CARE EITHER WAY NOW DESPISE YOU.
I'M NOT HERE TO MAKE FRIENDS, GENERAL. BEATING THE NAZIS IS THE ONLY THING THAT MATTERS TO ME.
THAT'S WHAT I LIKE TO HEAR, CAPTAIN.
OPERATION CRUSADER WILL LAUNCH ON 19 NOVEMBER. WILL YOU BE READY BY THEN?
WE'LL HAVE TO GO IN A FEW DAYS EARLIER, BUT YES, WE'LL BE READY, GENERAL.
I'VE PLANNED SEVERAL RAIDS AROUND GAZALA AND TMIMI. THAT WAY, ENEMY AIR FORCES WILL BE GROUNDED BEFORE THE ATTACK EVEN BEGINS.
HMMM ... IT WILL CERTAINLY HELP. THIS OFFENSIVE IS CRUCIAL AND WILL ALLOW US TO RETAKE TOBRUK AND DRIVE ROMMEL FAR AWAY FROM EGYPT.
WITHOUT HIS PLANES, THE FOX WILL HAVE TO STAY IN HIS DEN, GENERAL.
MAY GOD HEAR YOU, DAVID.

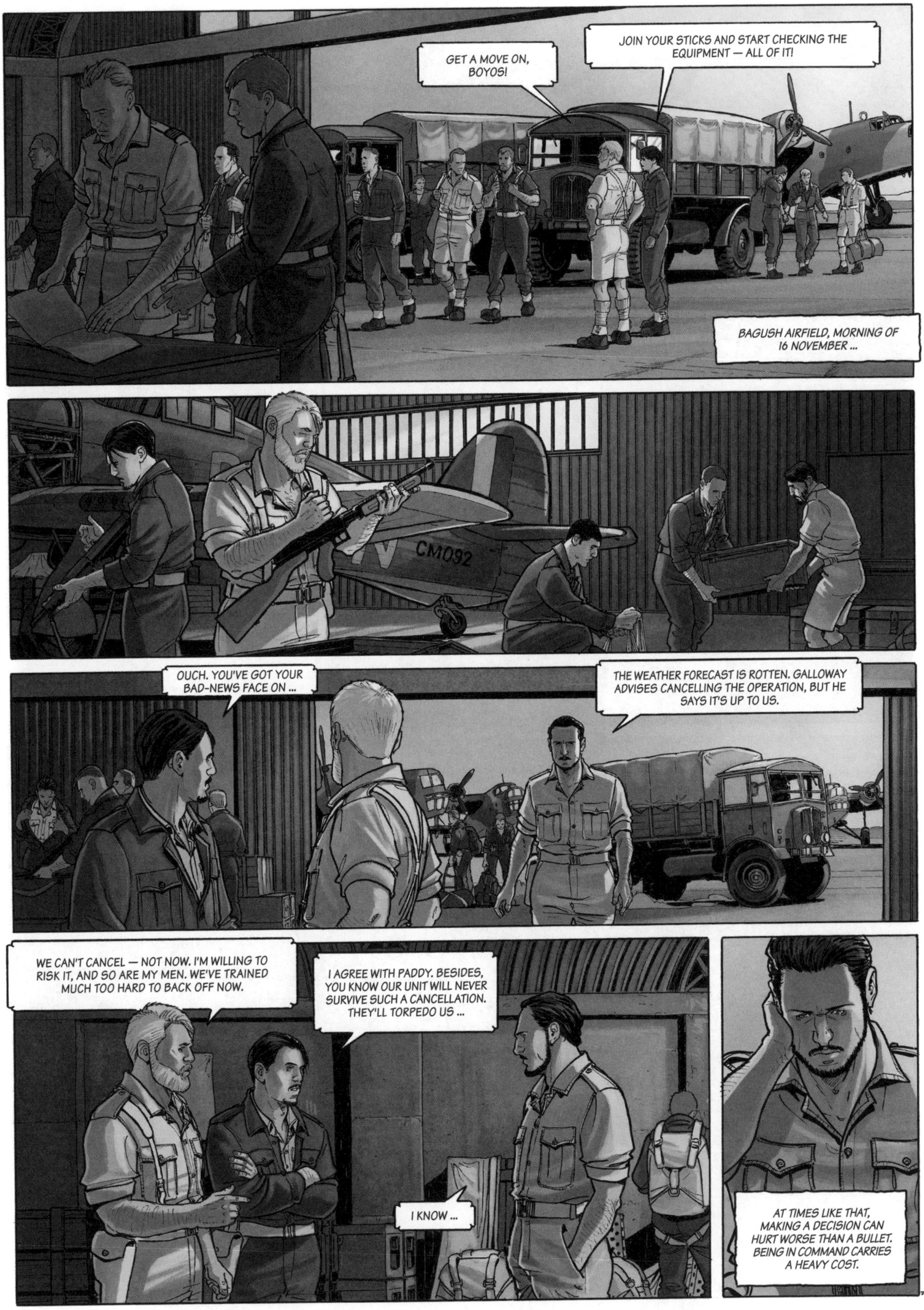
GET A MOVE ON, BOYOS!
JOIN YOUR STICKS AND START CHECKING THE EQUIPMENT — ALL OF IT!
BAGUSH AIRFIELD, MORNING OF 16 NOVEMBER ...
CM092
OUCH. YOU'VE GOT YOUR BAD-NEWS FACE ON ...
THE WEATHER FORECAST IS ROTTEN. GALLOWAY ADVISES CANCELLING THE OPERATION, BUT HE SAYS IT'S UP TO US.
WE CAN'T CANCEL — NOT NOW. I'M WILLING TO RISK IT, AND SO ARE MY MEN. WE'VE TRAINED MUCH TOO HARD TO BACK OFF NOW.
I AGREE WITH PADDY. BESIDES, YOU KNOW OUR UNIT WILL NEVER SURVIVE SUCH A CANCELLATION. THEY'LL TORPEDO US ...
I KNOW ...
AT TIMES LIKE THAT, MAKING A DECISION CAN HURT WORSE THAN A BULLET. BEING IN COMMAND CARRIES A HEAVY COST.

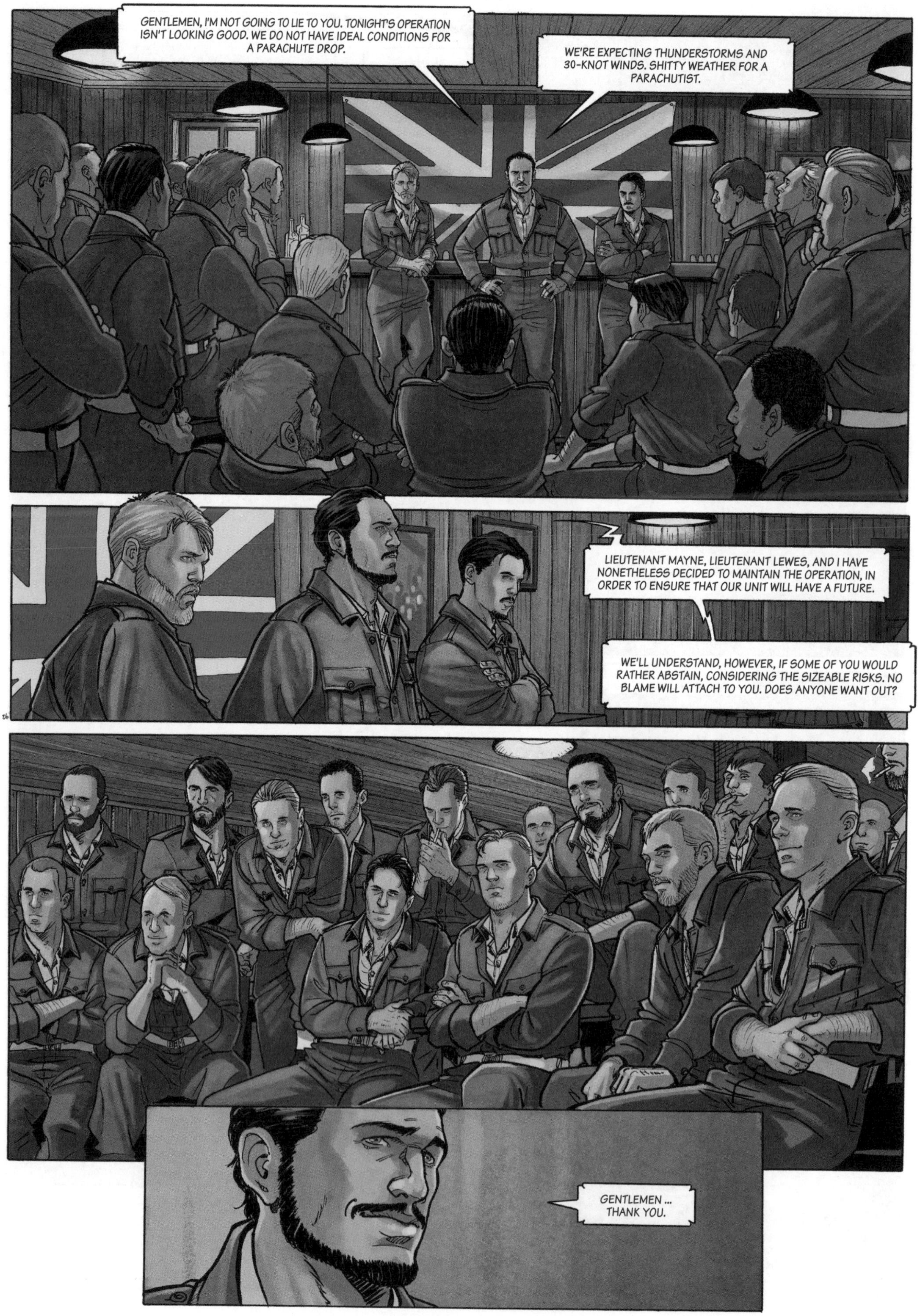
GENTLEMEN, I'M NOT GOING TO LIE TO YOU. TONIGHT'S OPERATION ISN'T LOOKING GOOD. WE DO NOT HAVE IDEAL CONDITIONS FOR A PARACHUTE DROP.
WE'RE EXPECTING THUNDERSTORMS AND 30-KNOT WINDS. SHITTY WEATHER FOR A PARACHUTIST.
LIEUTENANT MAYNE, LIEUTENANT LEWES, AND I HAVE NONETHELESS DECIDED TO MAINTAIN THE OPERATION, IN ORDER TO ENSURE THAT OUR UNIT WILL HAVE A FUTURE.
WE'LL UNDERSTAND, HOWEVER, IF SOME OF YOU WOULD RATHER ABSTAIN, CONSIDERING THE SIZEABLE RISKS. NO BLAME WILL ATTACH TO YOU. DOES ANYONE WANT OUT?
GENTLEMEN ... THANK YOU.

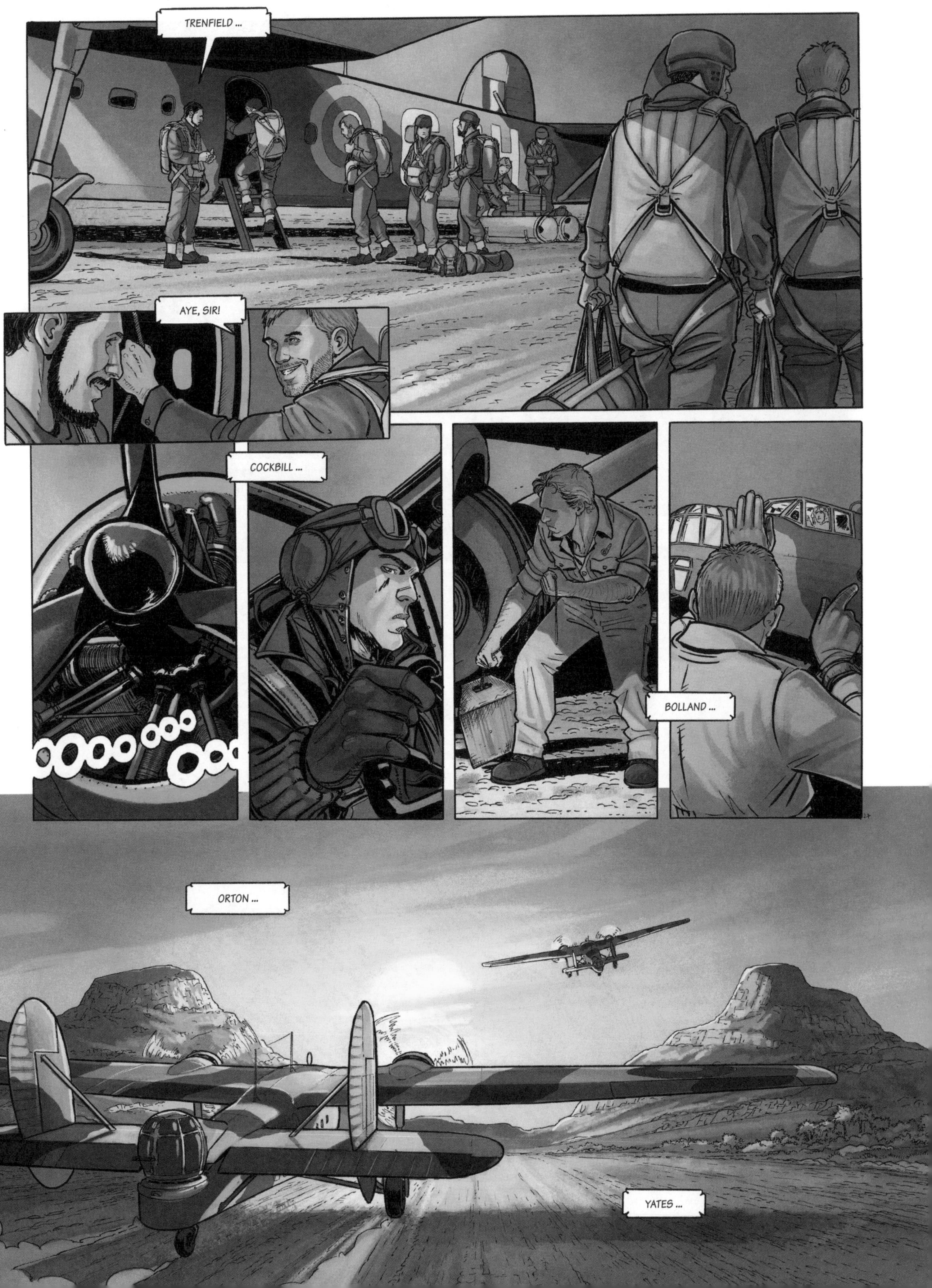
TRENFIELD ...
AYE, SIR!
COCKBILL ...
BOLLAND ...
ORTON ...
YATES ...

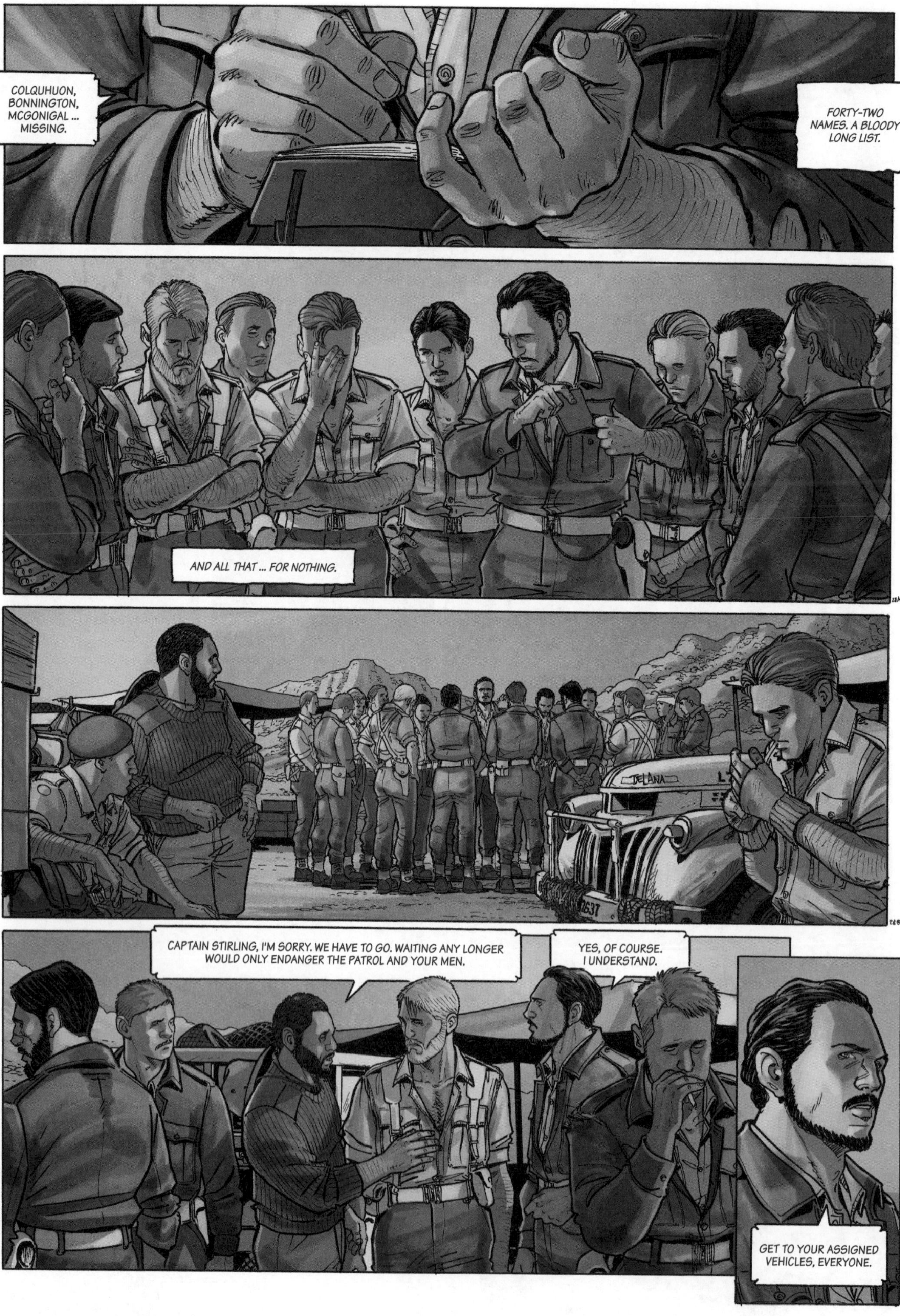
COLQUHUON, BONNINGTON, MCGONIGAL ... MISSING.
FORTY-TWO NAMES. A BLOODY LONG LIST.
AND ALL THAT ... FOR NOTHING.
CAPTAIN STIRLING, I'M SORRY. WE HAVE TO GO. WAITING ANY LONGER WOULD ONLY ENDANGER THE PATROL AND YOUR MEN.
YES, OF COURSE. I UNDERSTAND.
GET TO YOUR ASSIGNED VEHICLES, EVERYONE.

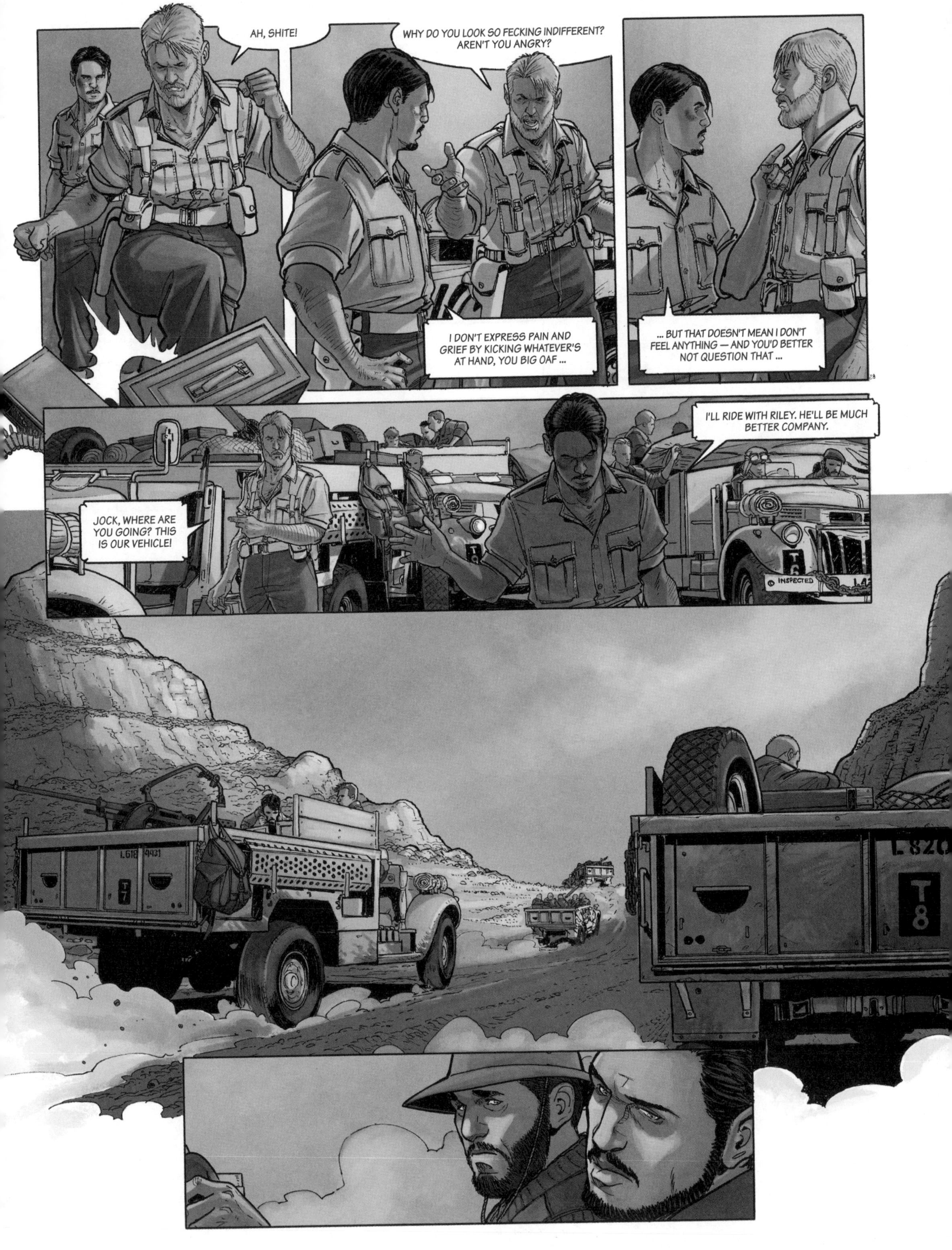
AH, SHITE!
WHY DO YOU LOOK SO FECKING INDIFFERENT? AREN'T YOU ANGRY?
I DON'T EXPRESS PAIN AND GRIEF BY KICKING WHATEVER'S AT HAND, YOU BIG OAF ...
... BUT THAT DOESN'T MEAN I DON'T FEEL ANYTHING — AND YOU'D BETTER NOT QUESTION THAT ...
I'LL RIDE WITH RILEY. HE'LL BE MUCH BETTER COMPANY.
JOCK, WHERE ARE YOU GOING? THIS IS OUR VEHICLE!
INSPECTED
L.618 4431
T7
L 820
T8

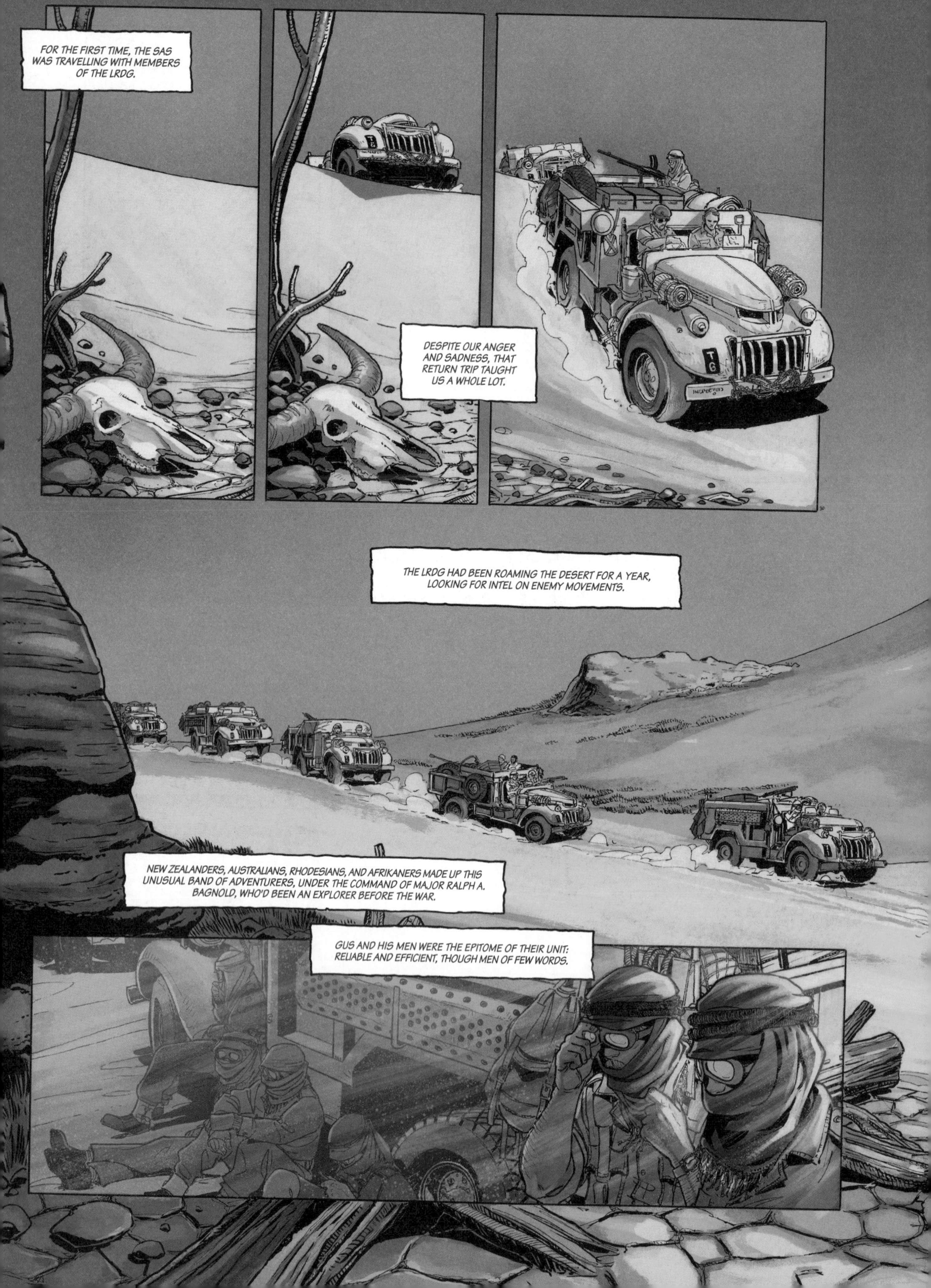
FOR THE FIRST TIME, THE SAS WAS TRAVELLING WITH MEMBERS OF THE LRDG.
DESPITE OUR ANGER AND SADNESS, THAT RETURN TRIP TAUGHT US A WHOLE LOT.
THE LRDG HAD BEEN ROAMING THE DESERT FOR A YEAR, LOOKING FOR INTEL ON ENEMY MOVEMENTS.
NEW ZEALANDERS, AUSTRALIANS, RHODESIANS, AND AFRIKANERS MADE UP THIS UNUSUAL BAND OF ADVENTURERS, UNDER THE COMMAND OF MAJOR RALPH A. BAGNOLD, WHO'D BEEN AN EXPLORER BEFORE THE WAR.
GUS AND HIS MEN WERE THE EPITOME OF THEIR UNIT: RELIABLE AND EFFICIENT, THOUGH MEN OF FEW WORDS.

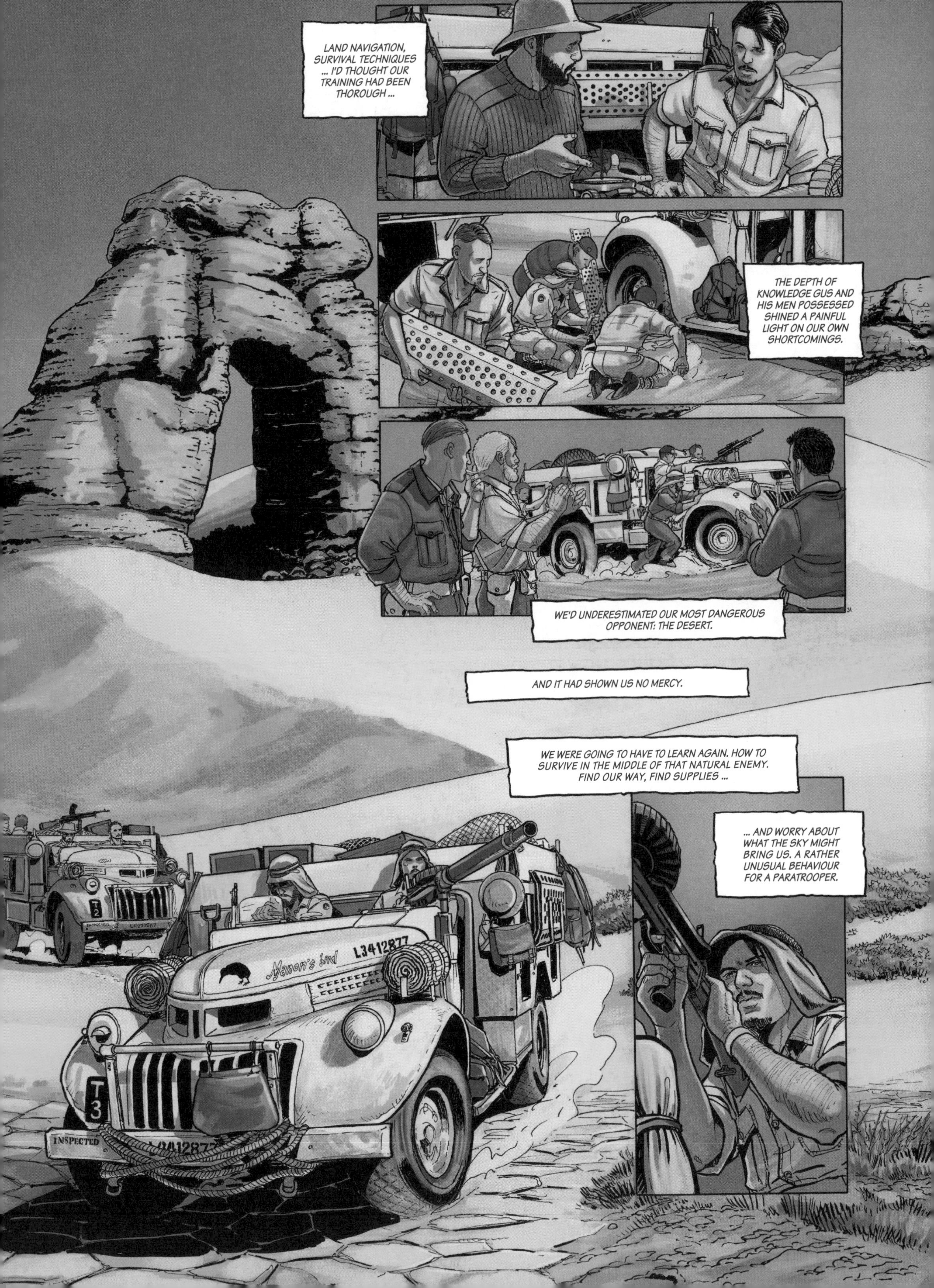
LAND NAVIGATION, SURVIVAL TECHNIQUES ... I'D THOUGHT OUR TRAINING HAD BEEN THOROUGH ...
THE DEPTH OF KNOWLEDGE GUS AND HIS MEN POSSESSED SHINED A PAINFUL LIGHT ON OUR OWN SHORTCOMINGS.
WE'D UNDERESTIMATED OUR MOST DANGEROUS OPPONENT: THE DESERT.
AND IT HAD SHOWN US NO MERCY.
WE WERE GOING TO HAVE TO LEARN AGAIN. HOW TO SURVIVE IN THE MIDDLE OF THAT NATURAL ENEMY. FIND OUR WAY, FIND SUPPLIES ...
... AND WORRY ABOUT WHAT THE SKY MIGHT BRING US. A RATHER UNUSUAL BEHAVIOUR FOR A PARATROOPER.
T2
Manon's bird
L3412877
T3
INSPECTED

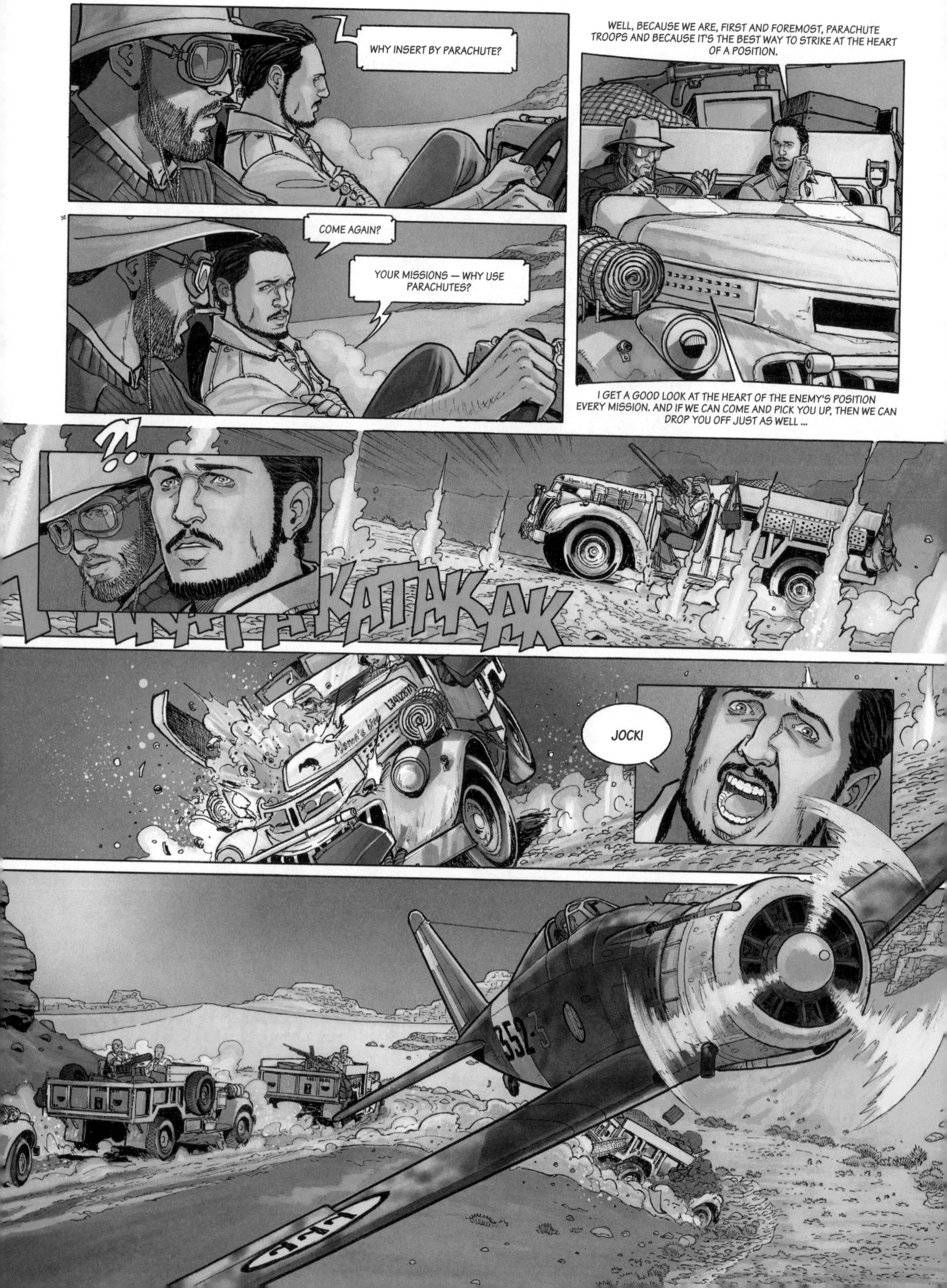
WHY INSERT BY PARACHUTE?
COME AGAIN?
YOUR MISSIONS — WHY USE PARACHUTES?
WELL, BECAUSE WE ARE, FIRST AND FOREMOST, PARACHUTE TROOPS AND BECAUSE IT'S THE BEST WAY TO STRIKE AT THE HEART OF A POSITION.
I GET A GOOD LOOK AT THE HEART OF THE ENEMY'S POSITION EVERY MISSION. AND IF WE CAN COME AND PICK YOU UP, THEN WE CAN DROP YOU OFF JUST AS WELL ...
?!
KATATAKAK
JOCK!
352-3

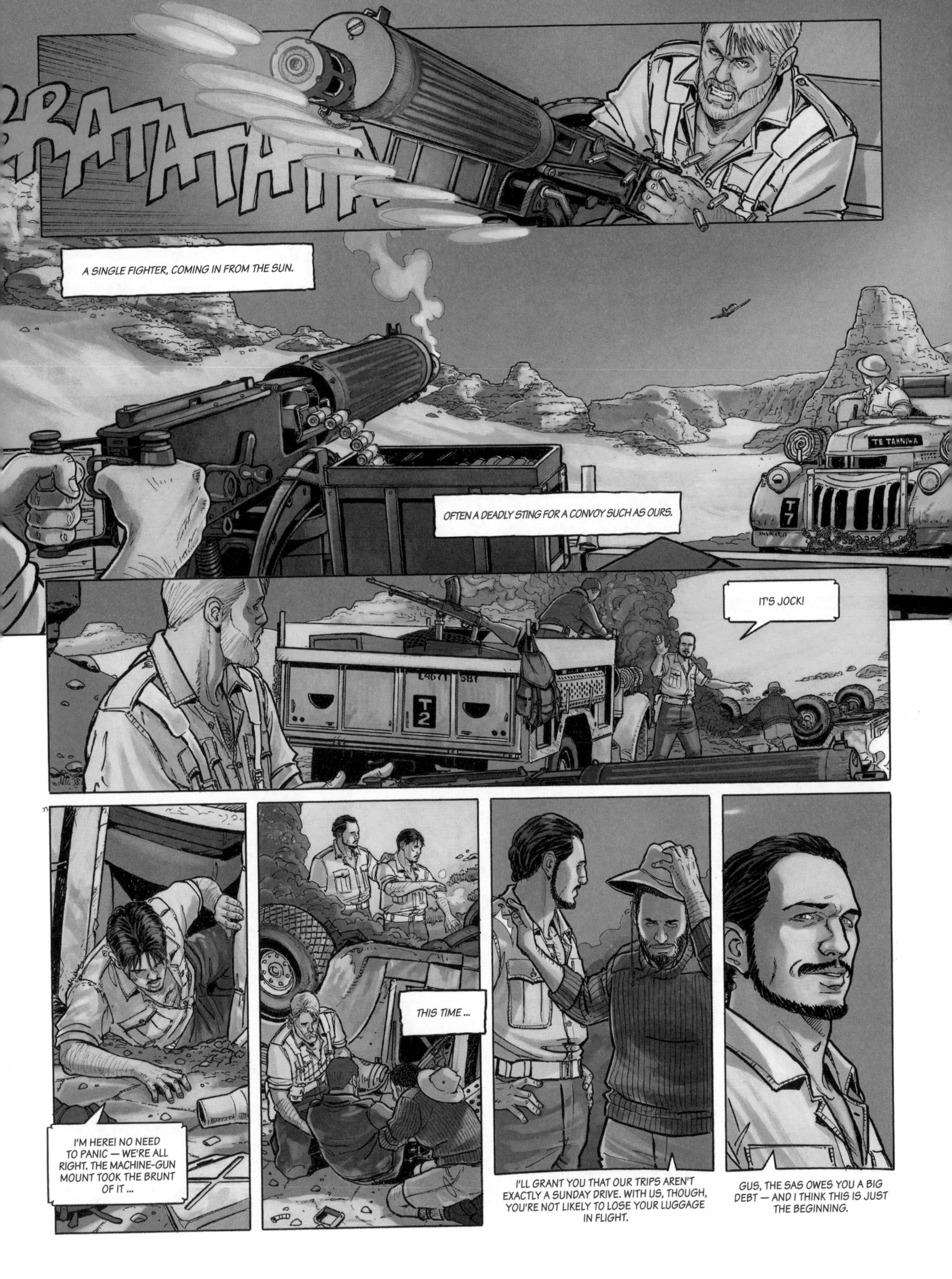
RATATATA
A SINGLE FIGHTER, COMING IN FROM THE SUN.
TE TAHNIWA
OFTEN A DEADLY STING FOR A CONVOY SUCH AS OURS.
IT'S JOCK!
I'M HERE! NO NEED TO PANIC — WE'RE ALL RIGHT. THE MACHINE-GUN MOUNT TOOK THE BRUNT OF IT ...
THIS TIME ...
I'LL GRANT YOU THAT OUR TRIPS AREN'T EXACTLY A SUNDAY DRIVE. WITH US, THOUGH, YOU'RE NOT LIKELY TO LOSE YOUR LUGGAGE IN FLIGHT.
GUS, THE SAS OWES YOU A BIG DEBT — AND I THINK THIS IS JUST THE BEGINNING.

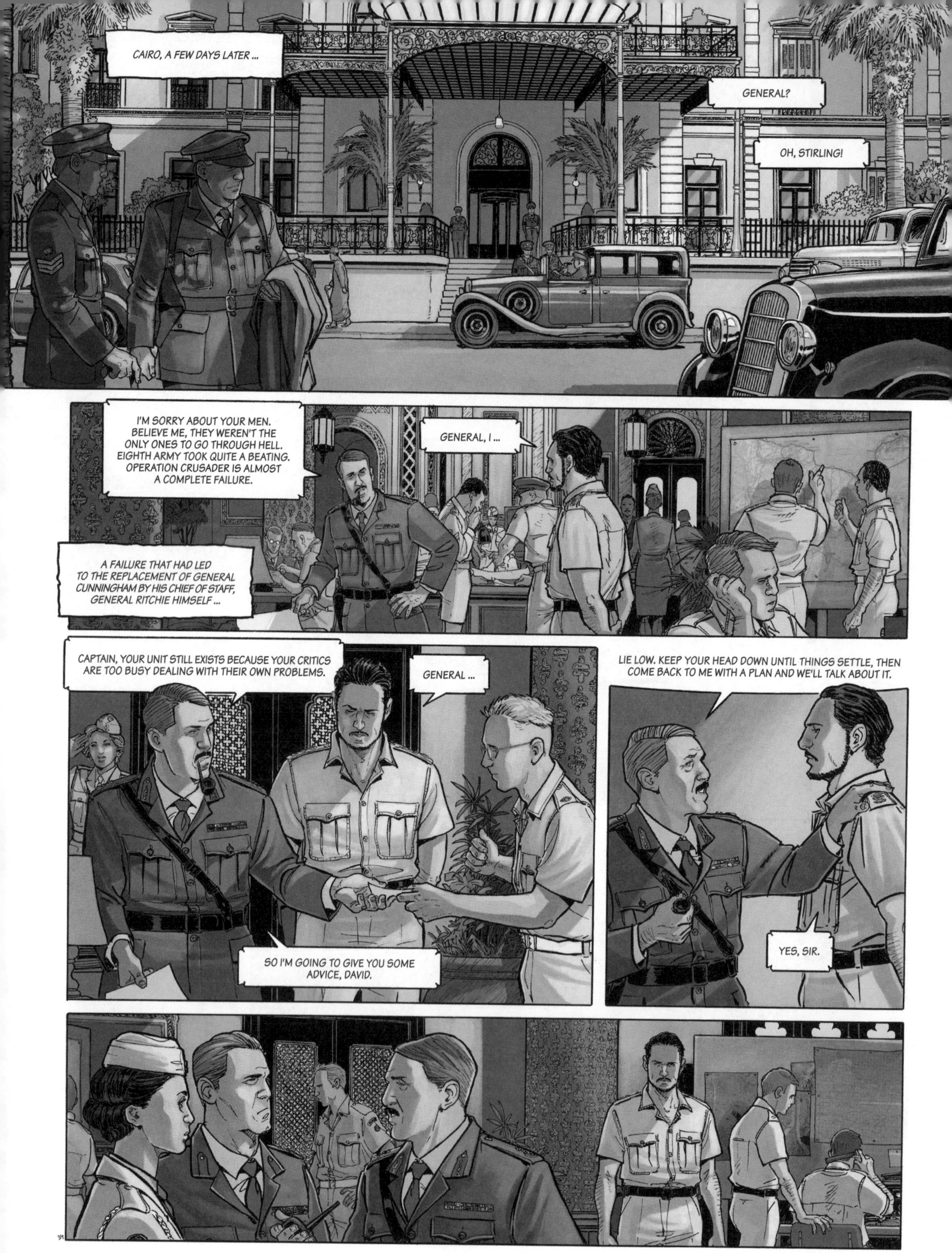

CAIRO, A FEW DAYS LATER ...
GENERAL?
OH, STIRLING!
I'M SORRY ABOUT YOUR MEN. BELIEVE ME, THEY WEREN'T THE ONLY ONES TO GO THROUGH HELL. EIGHTH ARMY TOOK QUITE A BEATING. OPERATION CRUSADER IS ALMOST A COMPLETE FAILURE.
GENERAL, I ...
A FAILURE THAT HAD LED TO THE REPLACEMENT OF GENERAL CUNNINGHAM BY HIS CHIEF OF STAFF, GENERAL RITCHIE HIMSELF ...
CAPTAIN, YOUR UNIT STILL EXISTS BECAUSE YOUR CRITICS ARE TOO BUSY DEALING WITH THEIR OWN PROBLEMS.
GENERAL ...
SO I'M GOING TO GIVE YOU SOME ADVICE, DAVID.
LIE LOW. KEEP YOUR HEAD DOWN UNTIL THINGS SETTLE, THEN COME BACK TO ME WITH A PLAN AND WE'LL TALK ABOUT IT.
YES, SIR.

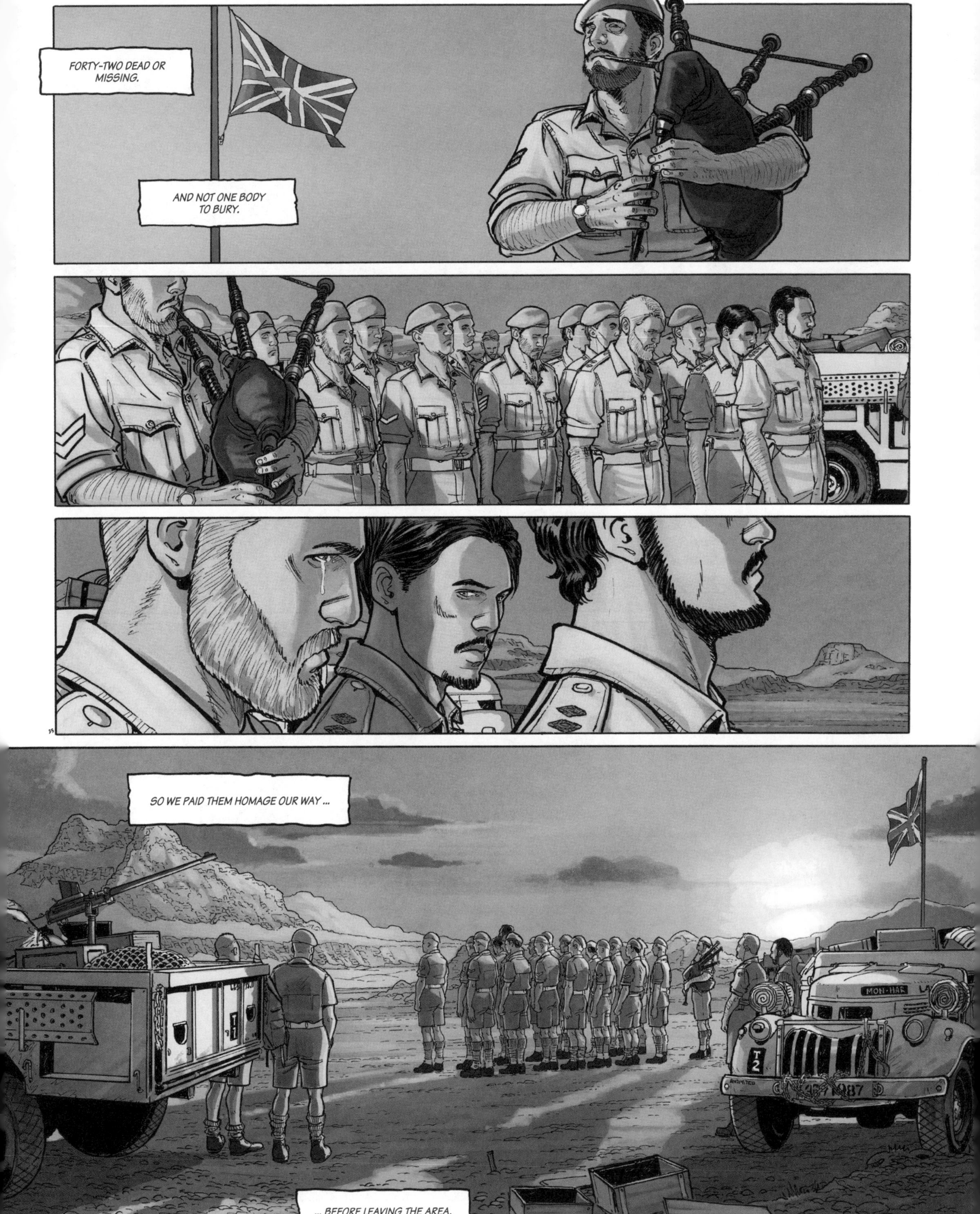
FORTY-TWO DEAD OR MISSING.
AND NOT ONE BODY TO BURY.
SO WE PAID THEM HOMAGE OUR WAY ...
... BEFORE LEAVING THE AREA.

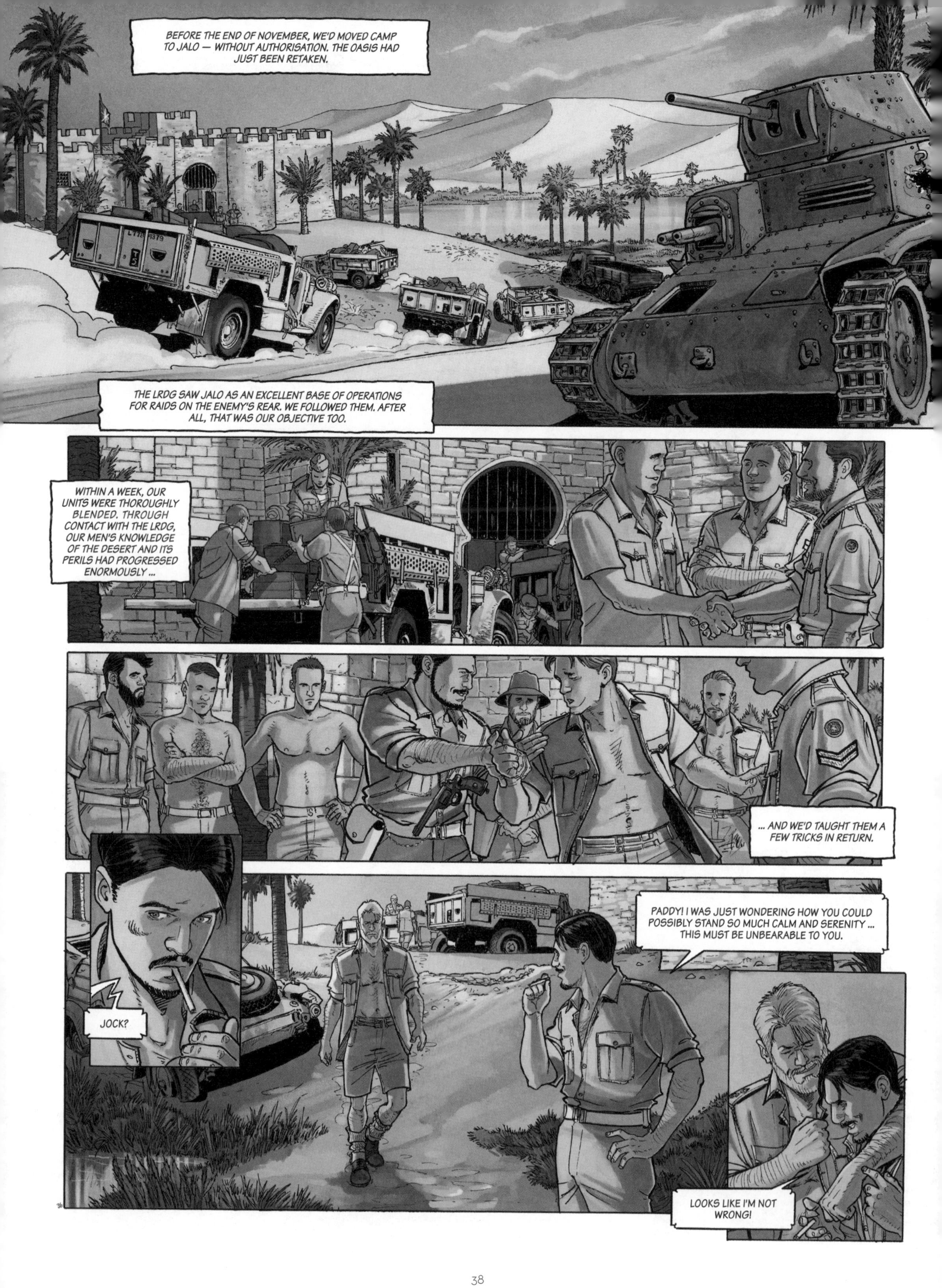
BEFORE THE END OF NOVEMBER, WE'D MOVED CAMP TO JALO — WITHOUT AUTHORISATION. THE OASIS HAD JUST BEEN RETAKEN.
THE LRDG SAW JALO AS AN EXCELLENT BASE OF OPERATIONS FOR RAIDS ON THE ENEMY'S REAR. WE FOLLOWED THEM. AFTER ALL, THAT WAS OUR OBJECTIVE TOO.
WITHIN A WEEK, OUR UNITS WERE THOROUGHLY BLENDED. THROUGH CONTACT WITH THE LRDG, OUR MEN'S KNOWLEDGE OF THE DESERT AND ITS PERILS HAD PROGRESSED ENORMOUSLY ...
... AND WE'D TAUGHT THEM A FEW TRICKS IN RETURN.
JOCK?
PADDY! I WAS JUST WONDERING HOW YOU COULD POSSIBLY STAND SO MUCH CALM AND SERENITY ... THIS MUST BE UNBEARABLE TO YOU.
LOOKS LIKE I'M NOT WRONG!

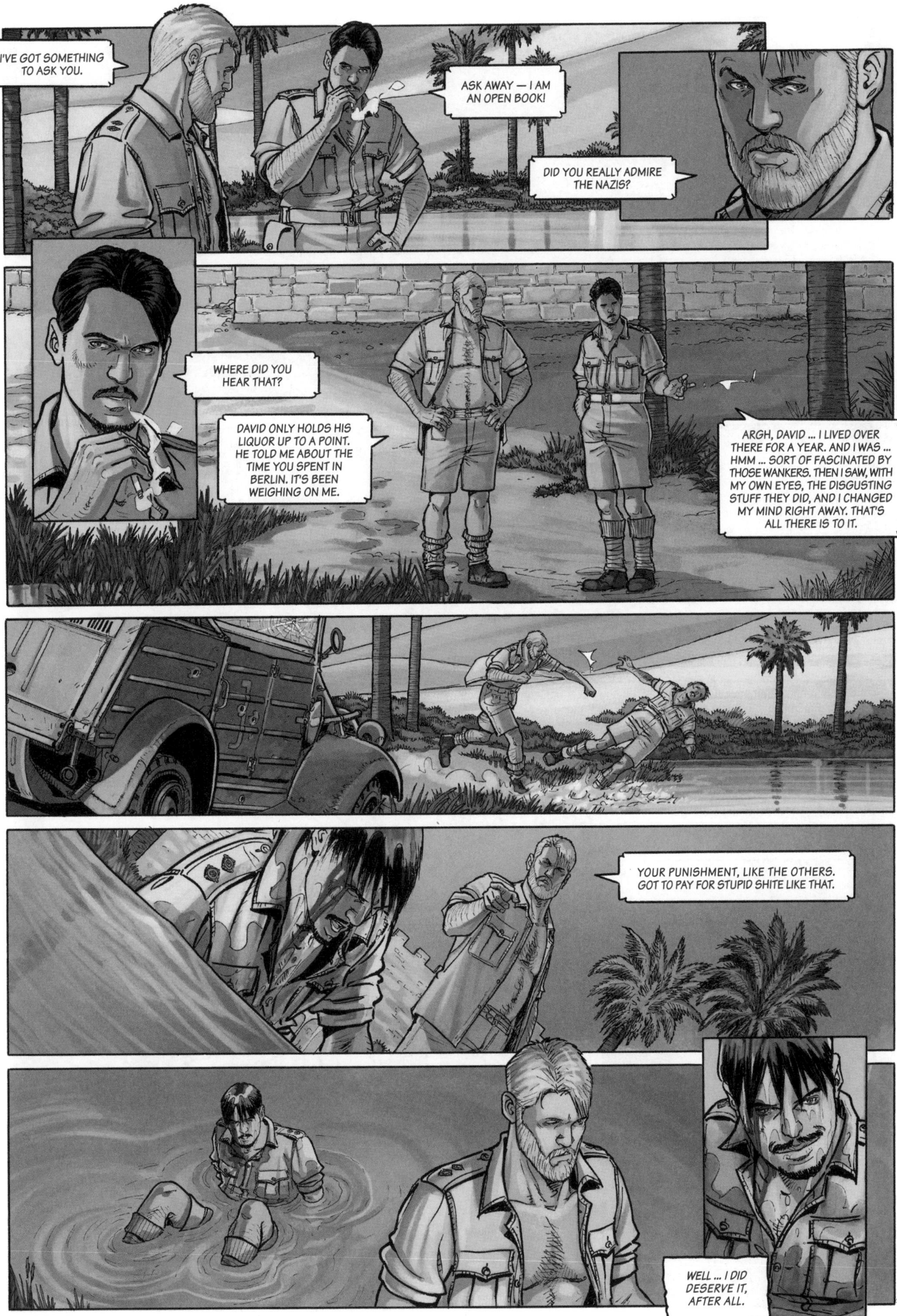
I'VE GOT SOMETHING TO ASK YOU.
ASK AWAY — I AM AN OPEN BOOK!
DID YOU REALLY ADMIRE THE NAZIS?
WHERE DID YOU HEAR THAT?
DAVID ONLY HOLDS HIS LIQUOR UP TO A POINT. HE TOLD ME ABOUT THE TIME YOU SPENT IN BERLIN. IT'S BEEN WEIGHING ON ME.
ARGH, DAVID ... I LIVED OVER THERE FOR A YEAR. AND I WAS ... HMM ... SORT OF FASCINATED BY THOSE WANKERS. THEN I SAW, WITH MY OWN EYES, THE DISGUSTING STUFF THEY DID, AND I CHANGED MY MIND RIGHT AWAY. THAT'S ALL THERE IS TO IT.
YOUR PUNISHMENT, LIKE THE OTHERS. GOT TO PAY FOR STUPID SHITE LIKE THAT.
WELL ... I DID DESERVE IT, AFTER ALL.

8 DECEMBER, JALO OASIS ...

DAVID'S AND PADDY'S GROUPS WERE ABOUT TO LEAVE.

IT WAS HIGH TIME DAVID WAS OFF.

ITINERARIES, TARGETS, TIMETABLES ... ANXIETY HAD TURNED HIM INTO A BROKEN RECORD ...

... AND, WHILE I COULD UNDERSTAND HIM, I WAS LONG PAST THE POINT WHERE I COULD BEAR IT ...

PADDY NEEDED TO GO TOO. HE WAS PACING THE CAMP LIKE A CAGED LION.

I WISH I COULD LEAVE AT THE SAME TIME AS YOU. HOW AM I SUPPOSED TO PULL YOUR ARSE OUT OF THE FIRE IF I'M NOT THERE?

NOT A CHANCE ...

... I REFUSE TO BE SLOWED DOWN BY SOME ITALIAN RATTLETRAP.

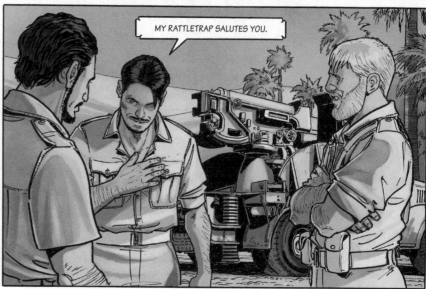

MY RATTLETRAP SALUTES YOU.

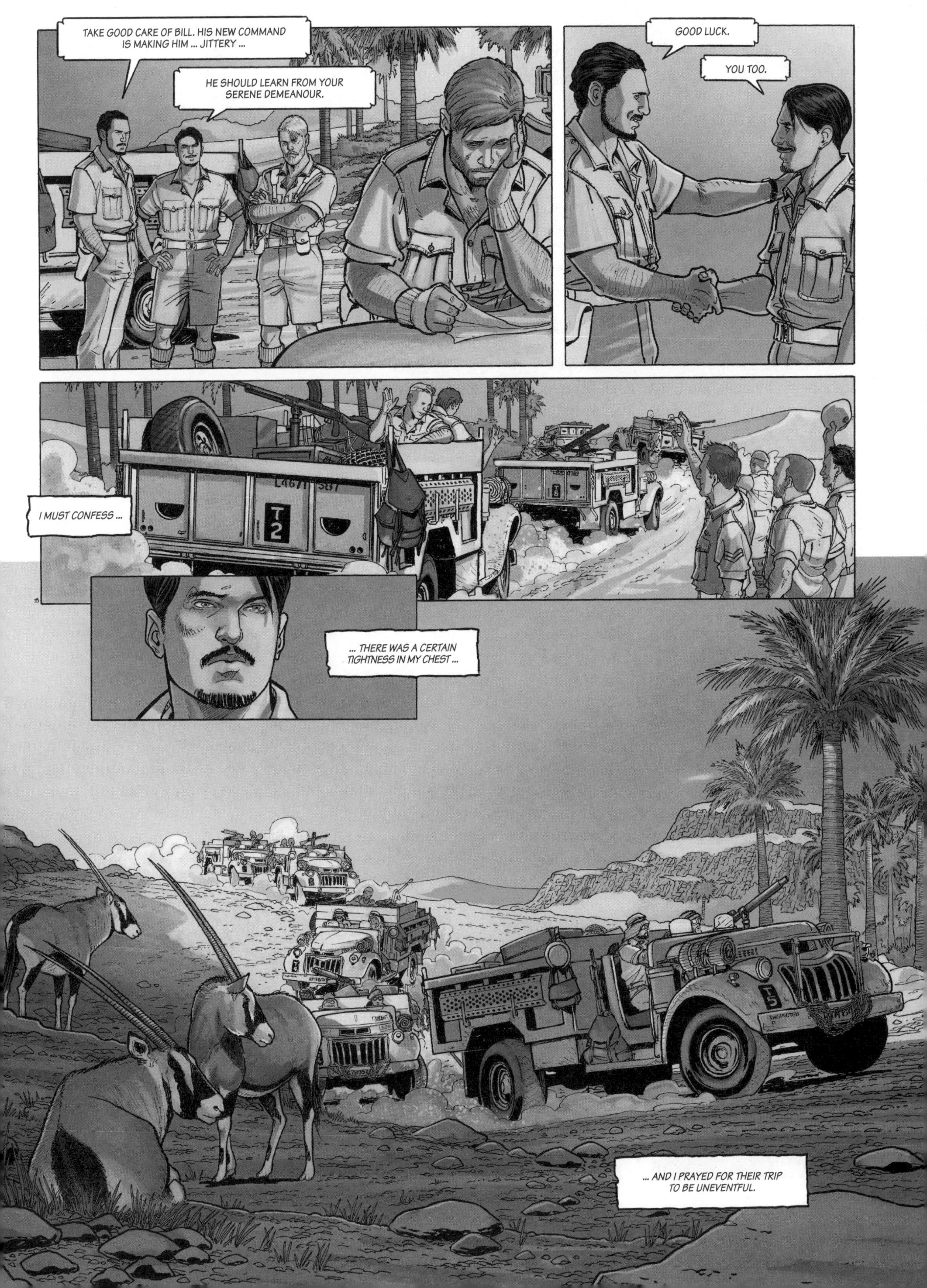
TAKE GOOD CARE OF BILL. HIS NEW COMMAND IS MAKING HIM ... JITTERY ...
HE SHOULD LEARN FROM YOUR SERENE DEMEANOUR.
GOOD LUCK.
YOU TOO.
I MUST CONFESS ...
... THERE WAS A CERTAIN TIGHTNESS IN MY CHEST ...
... AND I PRAYED FOR THEIR TRIP TO BE UNEVENTFUL.

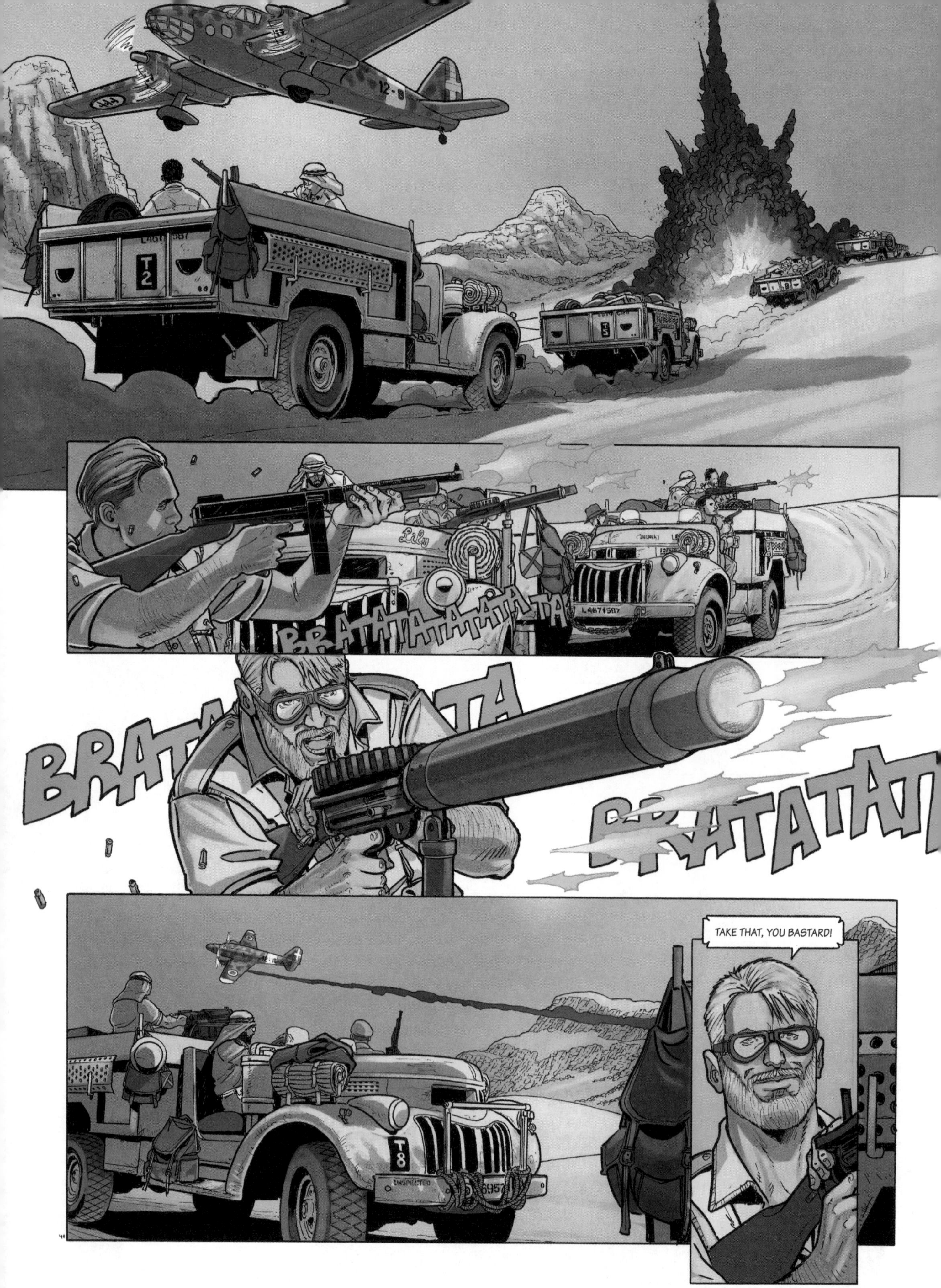
TAKE THAT, YOU BASTARD!

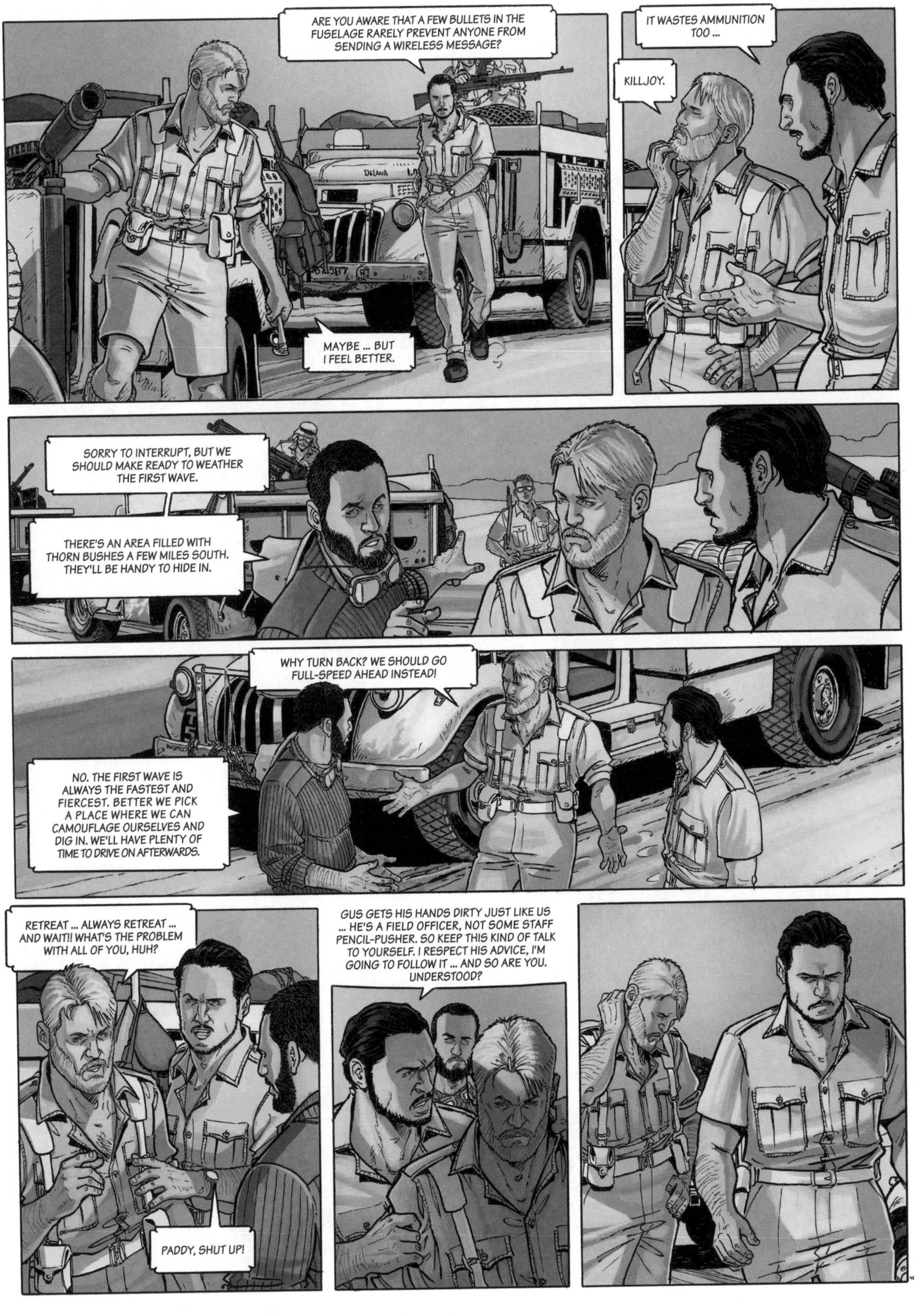
ARE YOU AWARE THAT A FEW BULLETS IN THE FUSELAGE RARELY PREVENT ANYONE FROM SENDING A WIRELESS MESSAGE?
MAYBE ... BUT I FEEL BETTER.
IT WASTES AMMUNITION TOO ...
KILLJOY.
SORRY TO INTERRUPT, BUT WE SHOULD MAKE READY TO WEATHER THE FIRST WAVE.
THERE'S AN AREA FILLED WITH THORN BUSHES A FEW MILES SOUTH. THEY'LL BE HANDY TO HIDE IN.
WHY TURN BACK? WE SHOULD GO FULL-SPEED AHEAD INSTEAD!
NO. THE FIRST WAVE IS ALWAYS THE FASTEST AND FIERCEST. BETTER WE PICK A PLACE WHERE WE CAN CAMOUFLAGE OURSELVES AND DIG IN. WE'LL HAVE PLENTY OF TIME TO DRIVE ON AFTERWARDS.
RETREAT ... ALWAYS RETREAT ... AND WAIT!! WHAT'S THE PROBLEM WITH ALL OF YOU, HUH?
PADDY, SHUT UP!
GUS GETS HIS HANDS DIRTY JUST LIKE US ... HE'S A FIELD OFFICER, NOT SOME STAFF PENCIL-PUSHER. SO KEEP THIS KIND OF TALK TO YOURSELF. I RESPECT HIS ADVICE, I'M GOING TO FOLLOW IT ... AND SO ARE YOU. UNDERSTOOD?

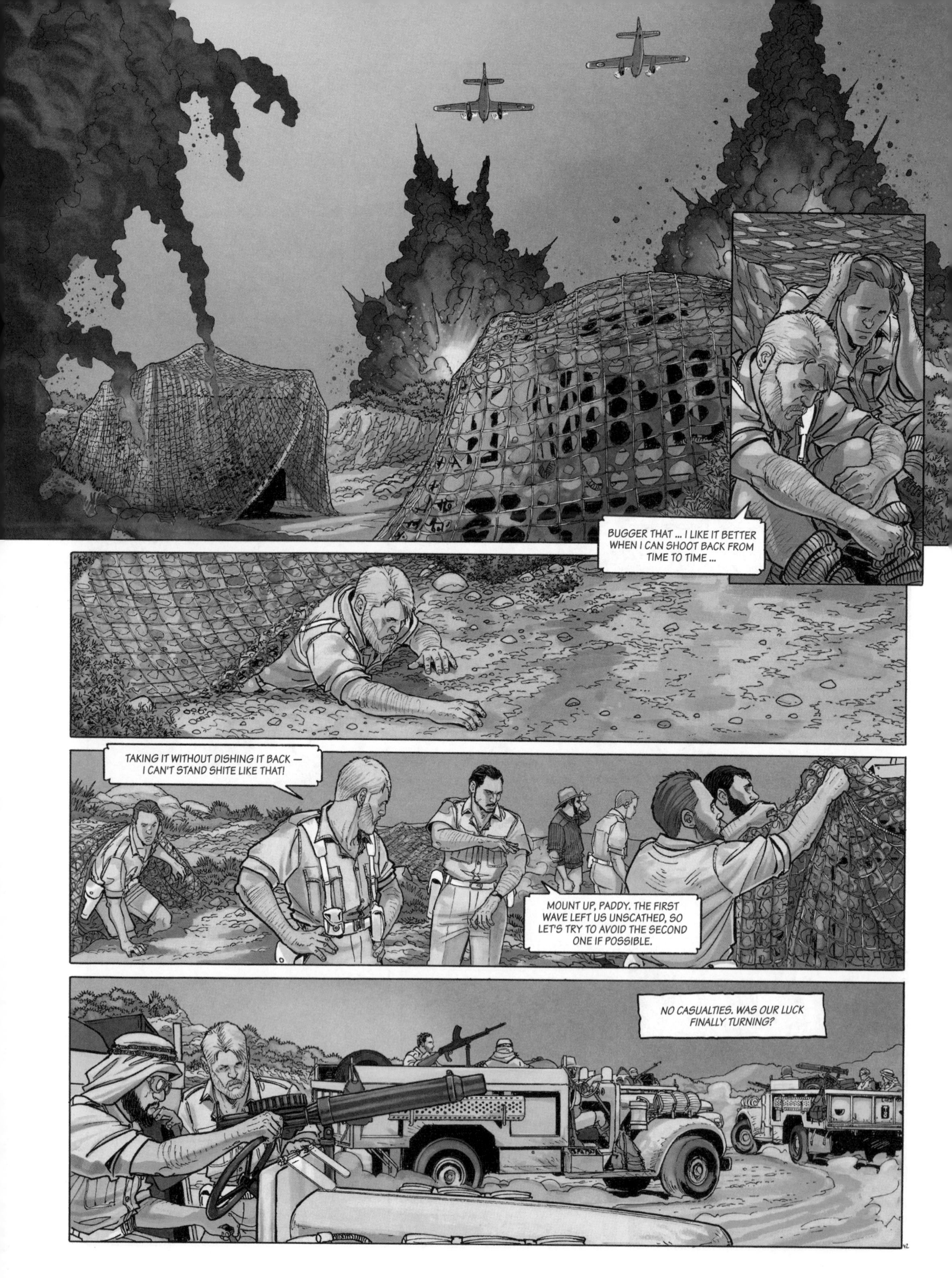
BUGGER THAT ... I LIKE IT BETTER WHEN I CAN SHOOT BACK FROM TIME TO TIME ...
TAKING IT WITHOUT DISHING IT BACK — I CAN'T STAND SHITE LIKE THAT!
MOUNT UP, PADDY. THE FIRST WAVE LEFT US UNSCATHED, SO LET'S TRY TO AVOID THE SECOND ONE IF POSSIBLE.
NO CASUALTIES. WAS OUR LUCK FINALLY TURNING?

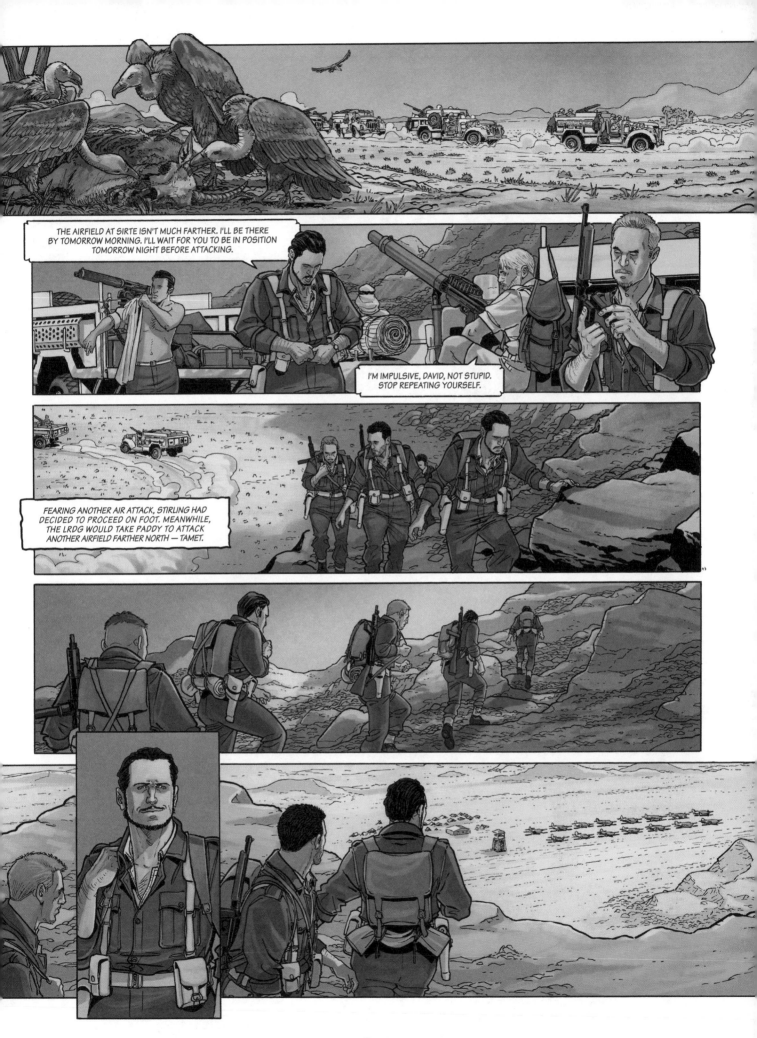

THE AIRFIELD AT SIRTE ISN'T MUCH FARTHER. I'LL BE THERE BY TOMORROW MORNING. I'LL WAIT FOR YOU TO BE IN POSITION TOMORROW NIGHT BEFORE ATTACKING.

I'M IMPULSIVE, DAVID, NOT STUPID. STOP REPEATING YOURSELF.

FEARING ANOTHER AIR ATTACK, STIRLING HAD DECIDED TO PROCEED ON FOOT. MEANWHILE, THE LRDG WOULD TAKE PADDY TO ATTACK ANOTHER AIRFIELD FARTHER NORTH — TAMET.

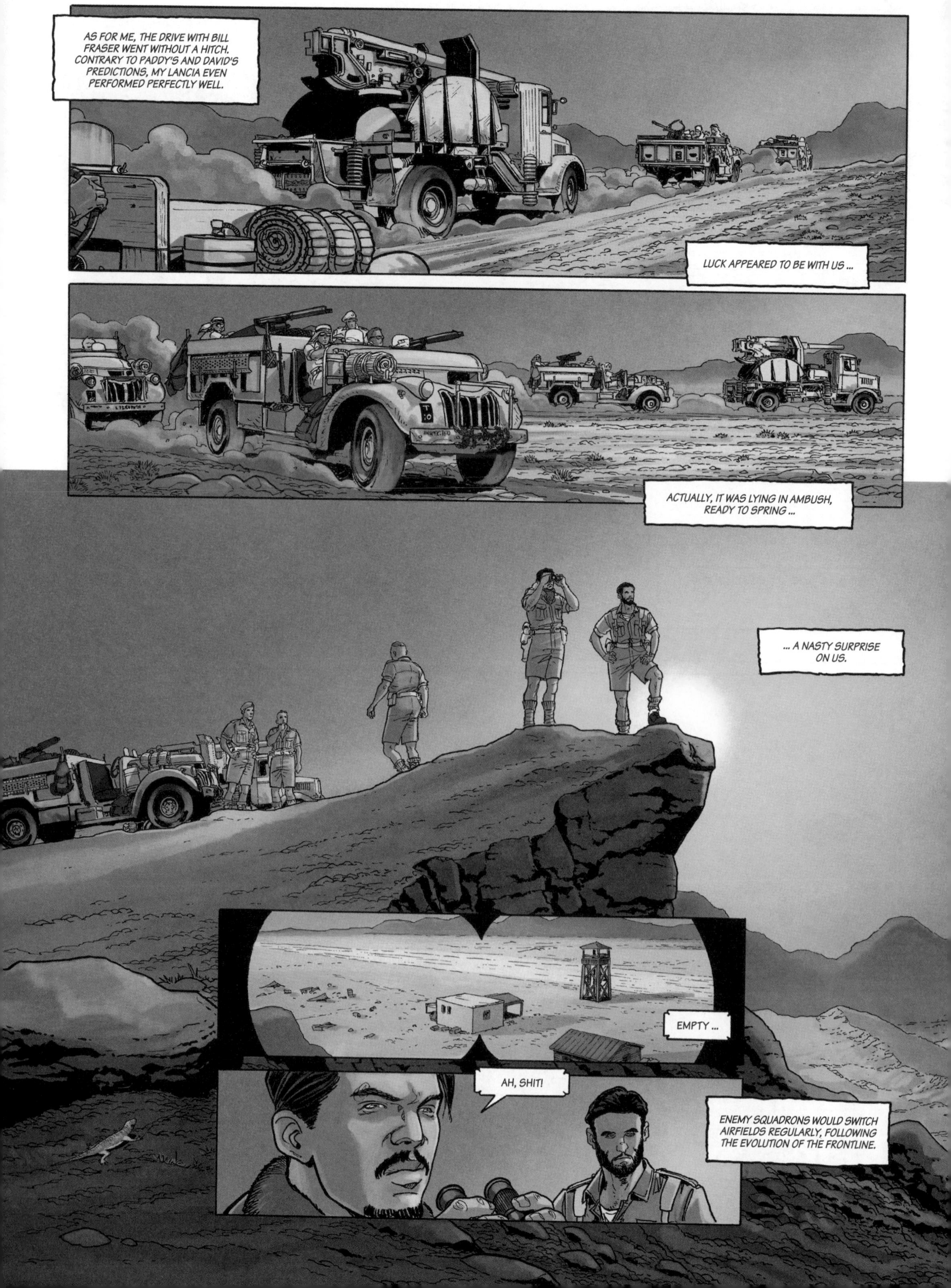

AS FOR ME, THE DRIVE WITH BILL FRASER WENT WITHOUT A HITCH. CONTRARY TO PADDY'S AND DAVID'S PREDICTIONS, MY LANCIA EVEN PERFORMED PERFECTLY WELL.
LUCK APPEARED TO BE WITH US ...
ACTUALLY, IT WAS LYING IN AMBUSH, READY TO SPRING ...
... A NASTY SURPRISE ON US.
EMPTY ...
AH, SHIT!
ENEMY SQUADRONS WOULD SWITCH AIRFIELDS REGULARLY, FOLLOWING THE EVOLUTION OF THE FRONTLINE.

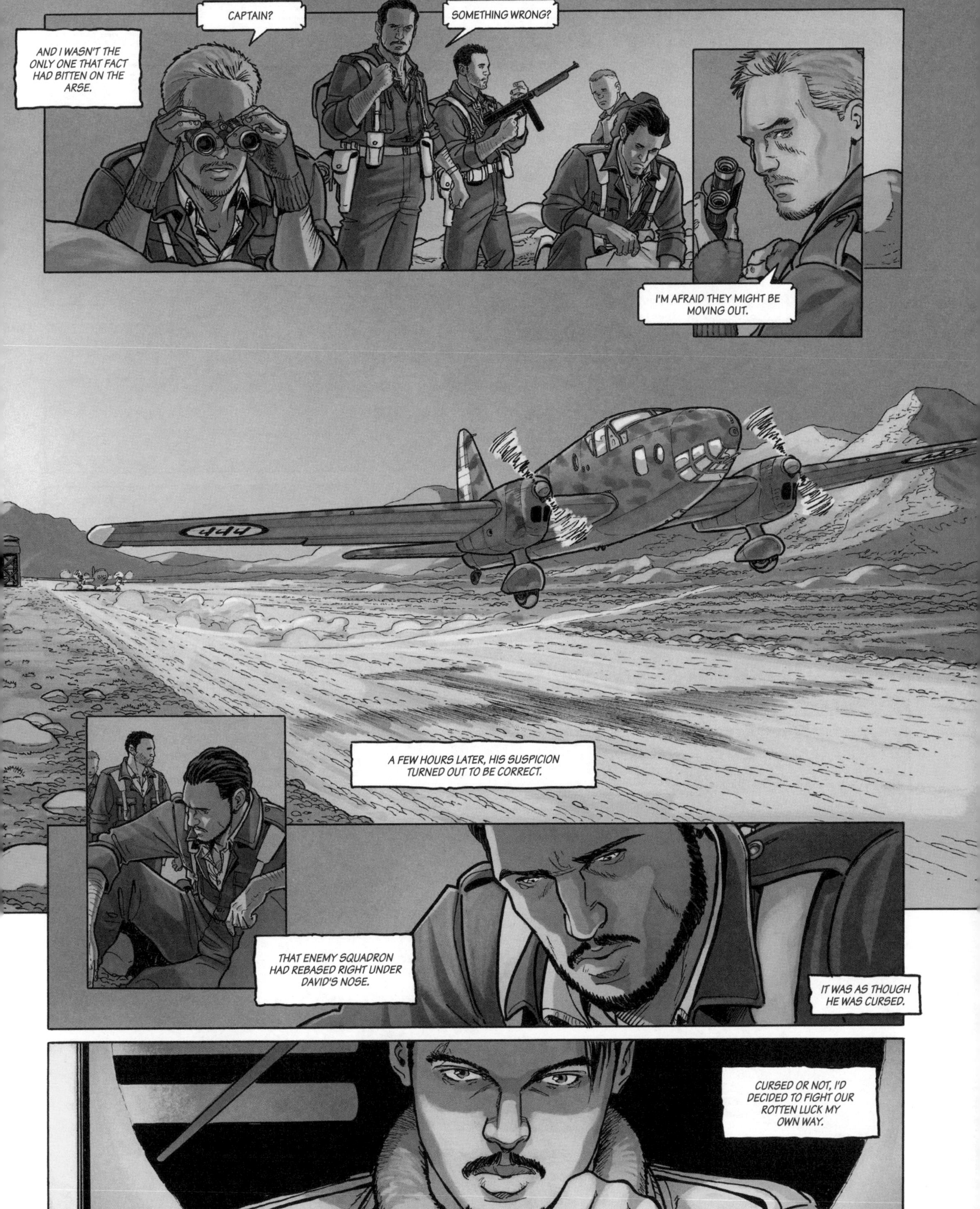
AND I WASN'T THE ONLY ONE THAT FACT HAD BITTEN ON THE ARSE.
CAPTAIN?
SOMETHING WRONG?
I'M AFRAID THEY MIGHT BE MOVING OUT.
A FEW HOURS LATER, HIS SUSPICION TURNED OUT TO BE CORRECT.
THAT ENEMY SQUADRON HAD REBASED RIGHT UNDER DAVID'S NOSE.
IT WAS AS THOUGH HE WAS CURSED.
CURSED OR NOT, I'D DECIDED TO FIGHT OUR ROTTEN LUCK MY OWN WAY.

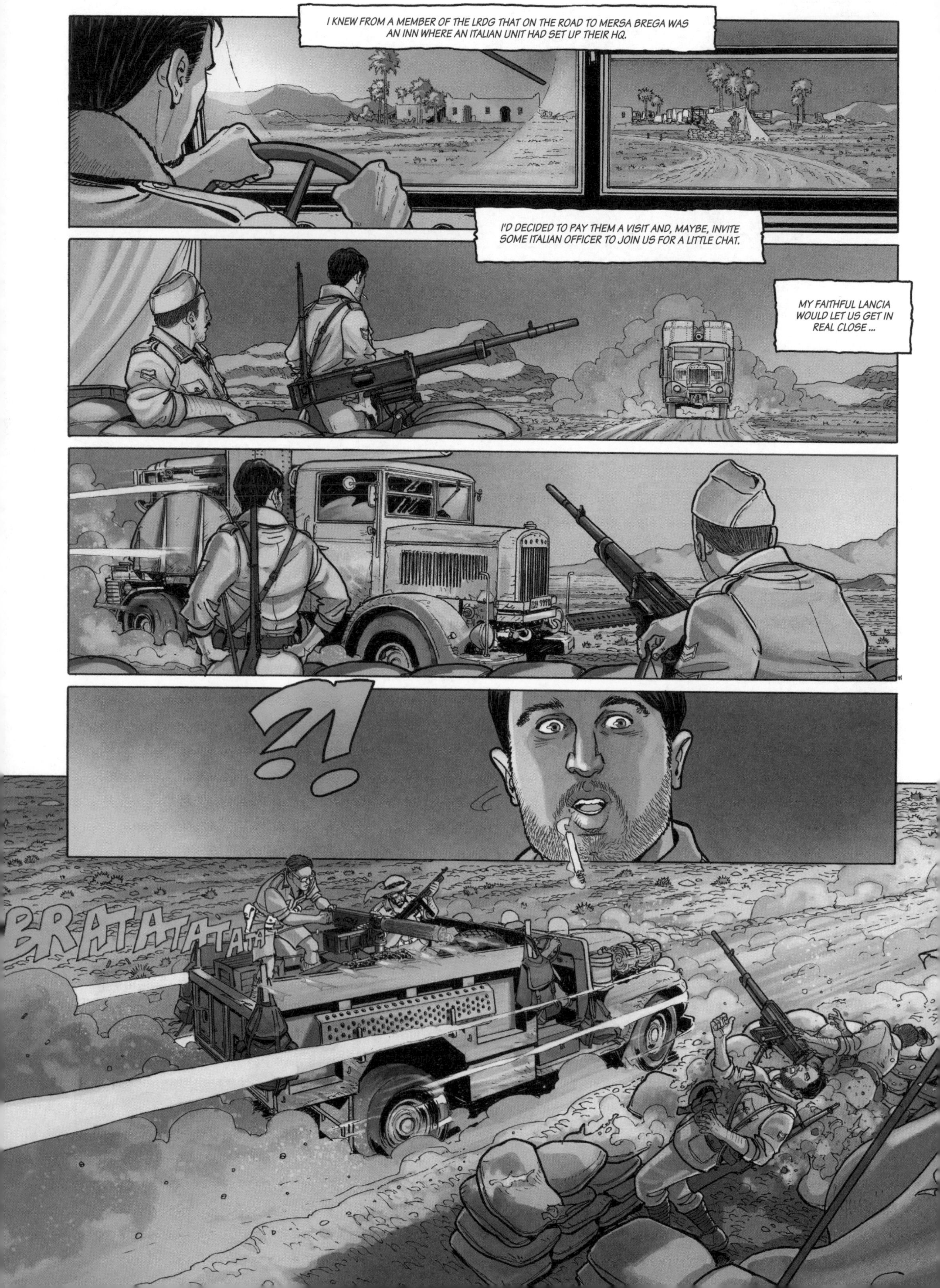
I KNEW FROM A MEMBER OF THE LRDG THAT ON THE ROAD TO MERSA BREGA WAS AN INN WHERE AN ITALIAN UNIT HAD SET UP THEIR HQ.
I'D DECIDED TO PAY THEM A VISIT AND, MAYBE, INVITE SOME ITALIAN OFFICER TO JOIN US FOR A LITTLE CHAT.
MY FAITHFUL LANCIA WOULD LET US GET IN REAL CLOSE ...
?!
BRATATATATATA

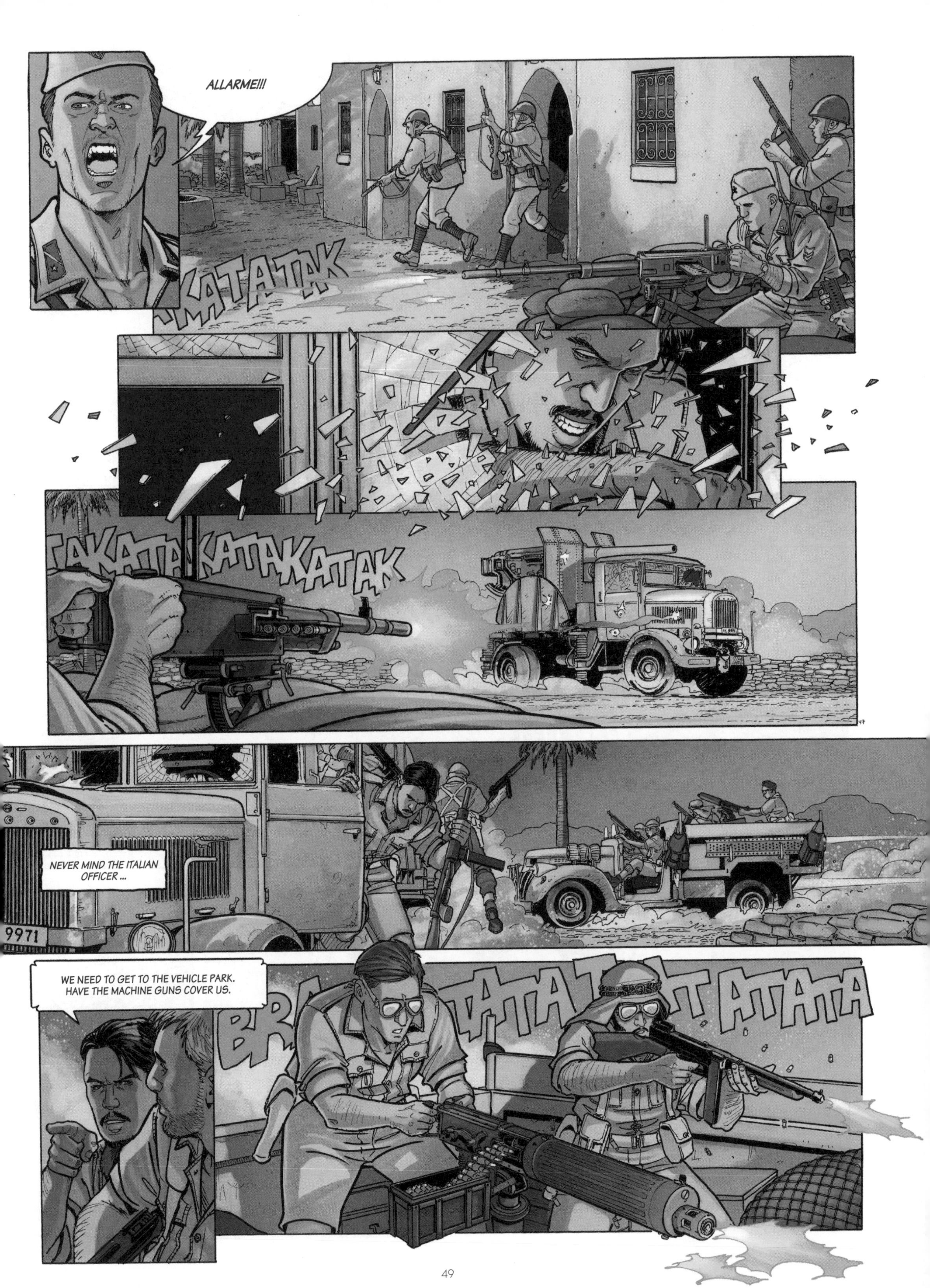

ALLARME!!!
KATATAK
TAKATA KATAKATAK
NEVER MIND THE ITALIAN OFFICER ...
WE NEED TO GET TO THE VEHICLE PARK. HAVE THE MACHINE GUNS COVER US.
BRATATATATATATA

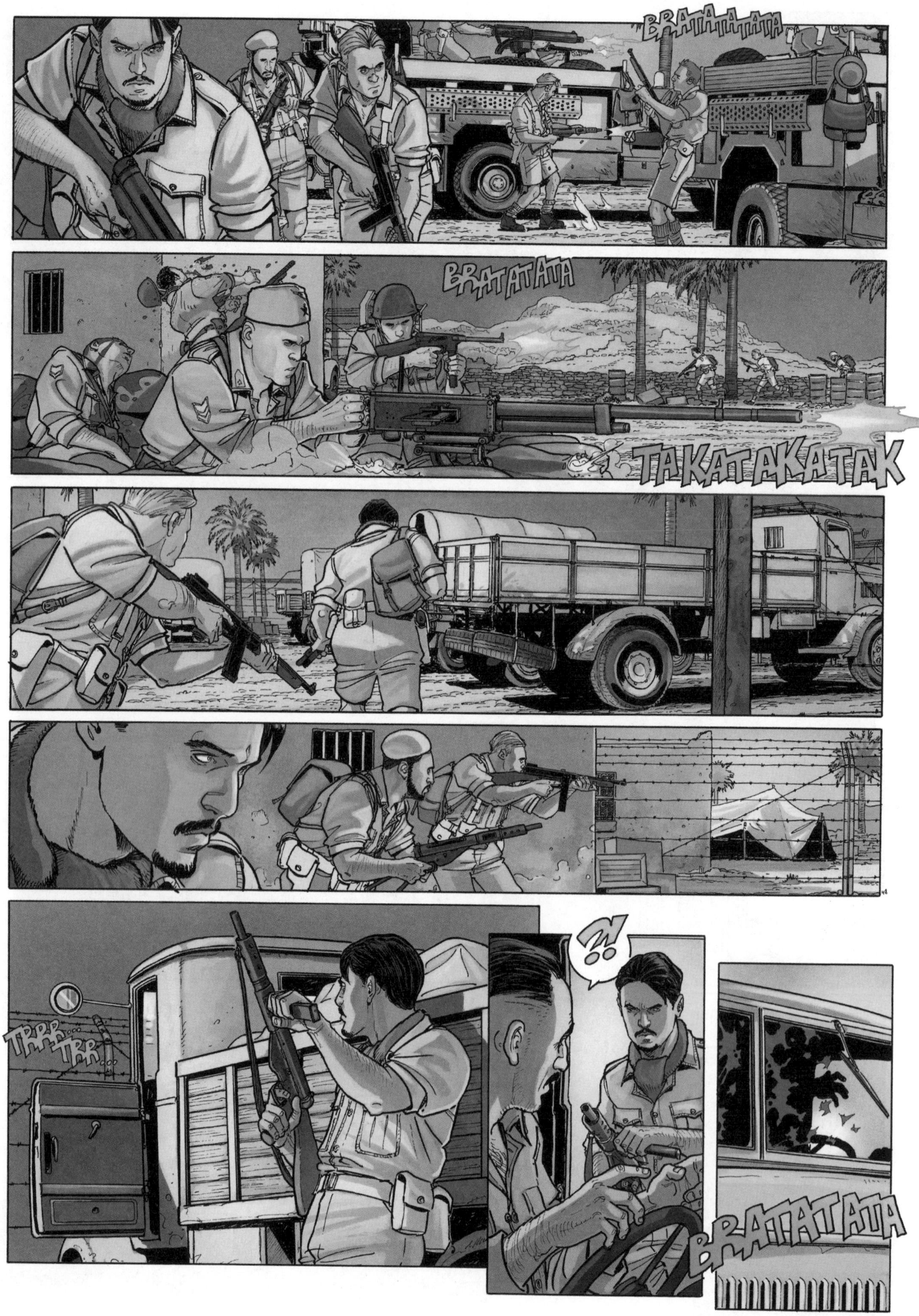
BRATATATATA
BRATATATA
TAKATAKATAK
TRRR...
TRR...
?!
BRATATATA

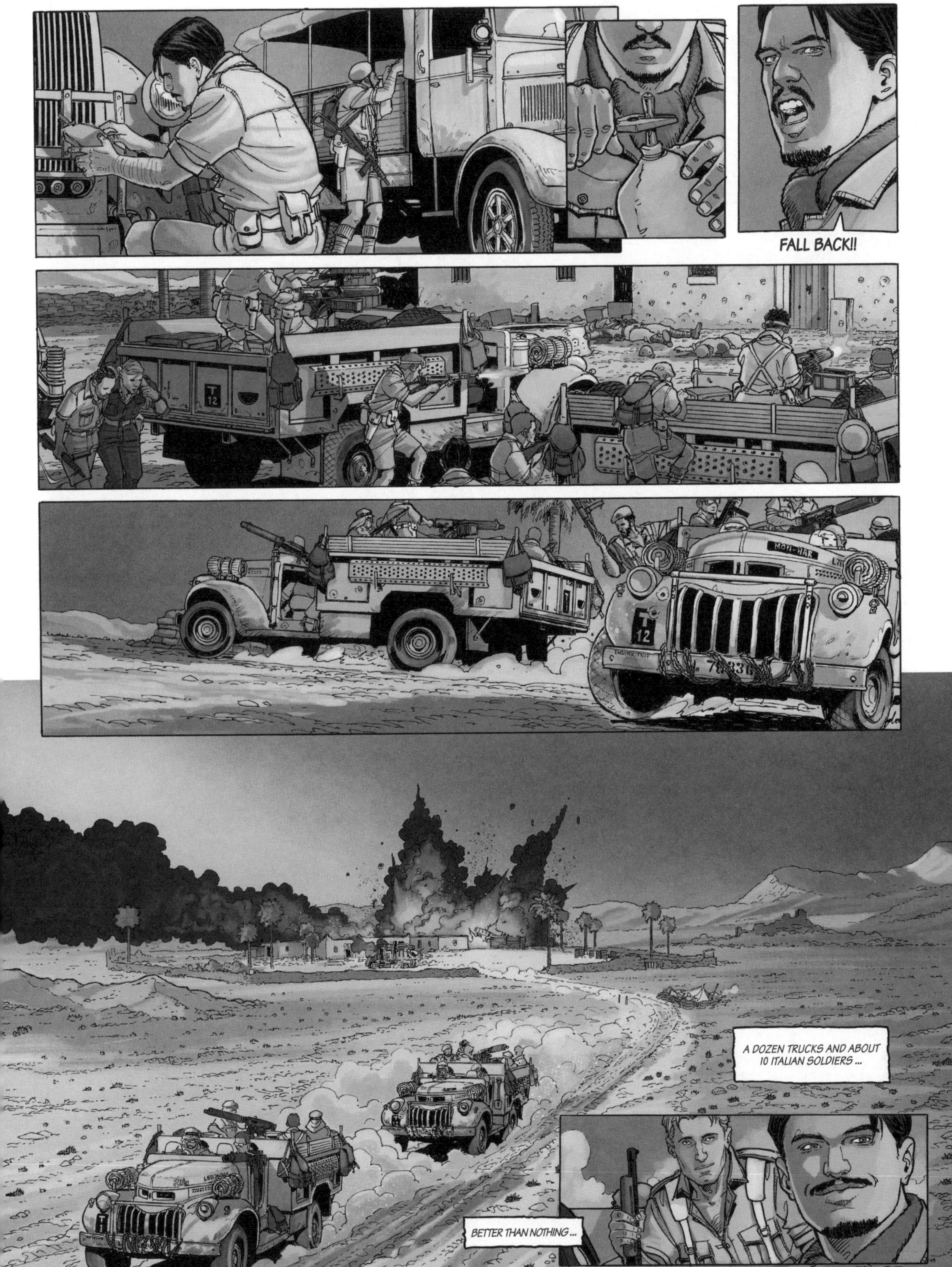
FALL BACK!!
A DOZEN TRUCKS AND ABOUT 10 ITALIAN SOLDIERS ...
BETTER THAN NOTHING ...

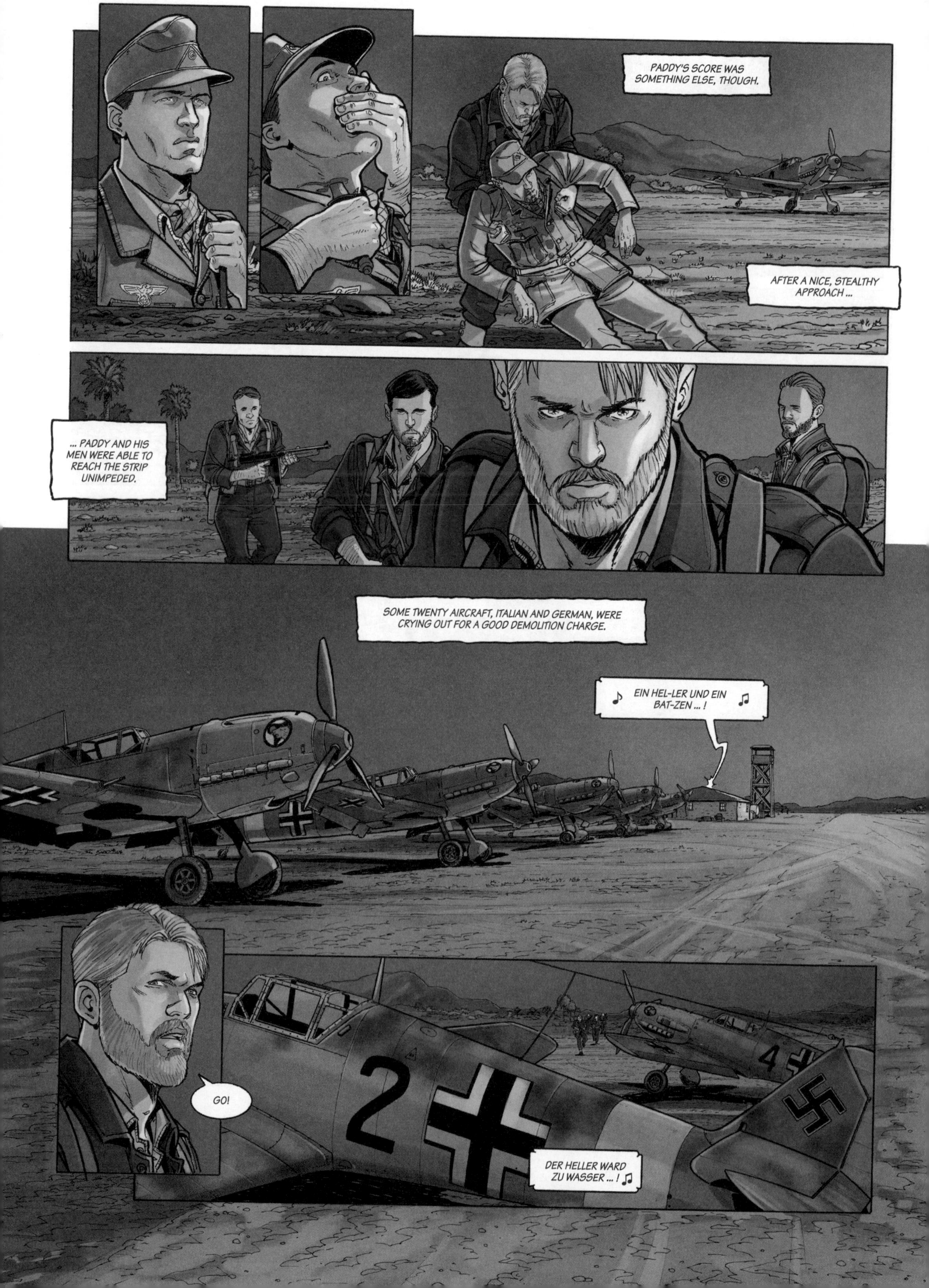
PADDY'S SCORE WAS SOMETHING ELSE, THOUGH.
AFTER A NICE, STEALTHY APPROACH ...
... PADDY AND HIS MEN WERE ABLE TO REACH THE STRIP UNIMPEDED.
SOME TWENTY AIRCRAFT, ITALIAN AND GERMAN, WERE CRYING OUT FOR A GOOD DEMOLITION CHARGE.
♪ EIN HEL-LER UND EIN BAT-ZEN ... ! ♫
GO!
DER HELLER WARD ZU WASSER ... ! ♫

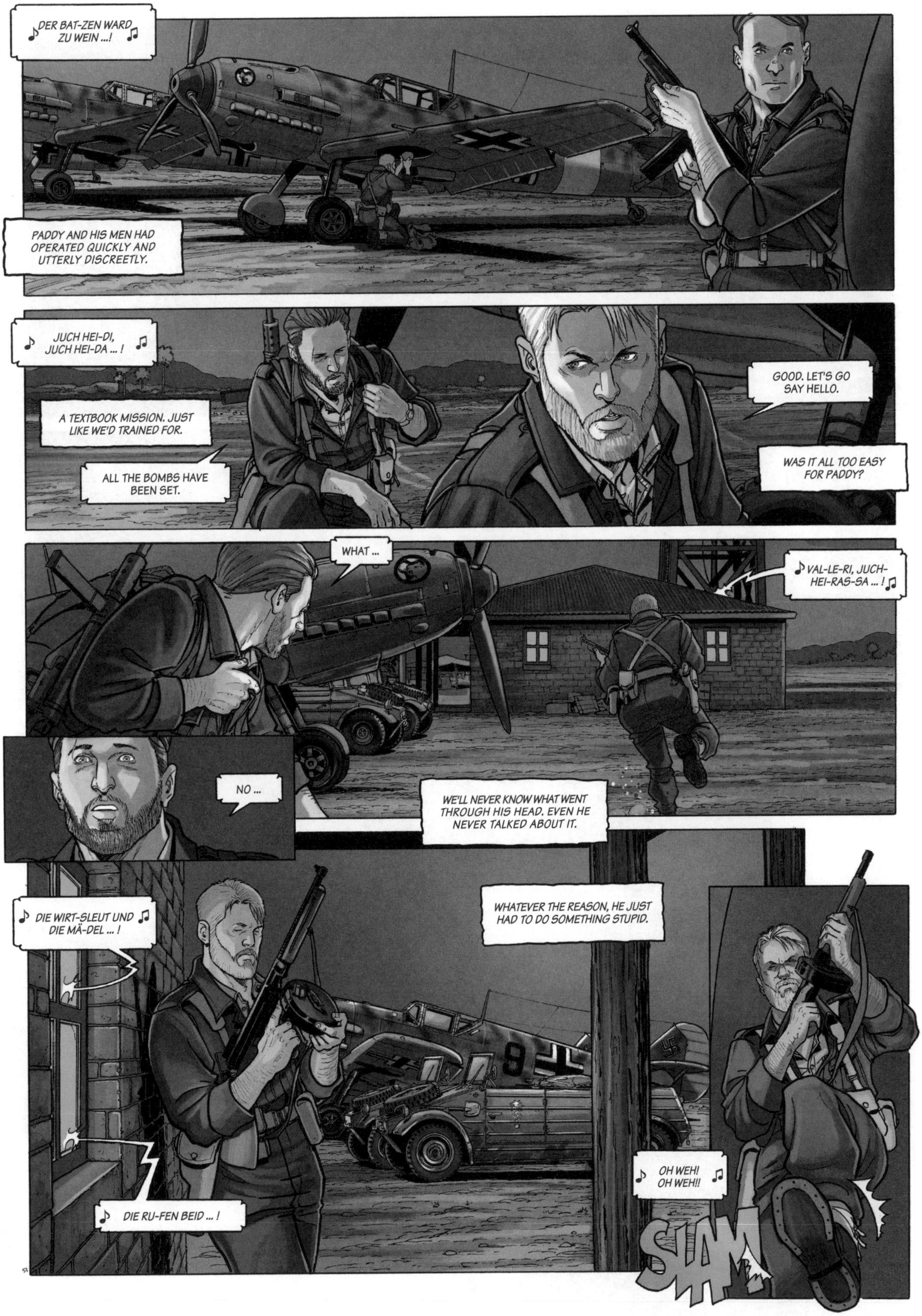

DER BAT-ZEN WARD ZU WEIN ...!
PADDY AND HIS MEN HAD OPERATED QUICKLY AND UTTERLY DISCREETLY.
JUCH HEI-DI, JUCH HEI-DA ... !
A TEXTBOOK MISSION. JUST LIKE WE'D TRAINED FOR.
ALL THE BOMBS HAVE BEEN SET.
GOOD. LET'S GO SAY HELLO.
WAS IT ALL TOO EASY FOR PADDY?
WHAT ...
VAL-LE-RI, JUCH-HEI-RAS-SA ... !
NO ...
WE'LL NEVER KNOW WHAT WENT THROUGH HIS HEAD. EVEN HE NEVER TALKED ABOUT IT.
DIE WIRT-SLEUT UND DIE MÄ-DEL ... !
WHATEVER THE REASON, HE JUST HAD TO DO SOMETHING STUPID.
DIE RU-FEN BEID ... !
OH WEH! OH WEH!!
SLAM

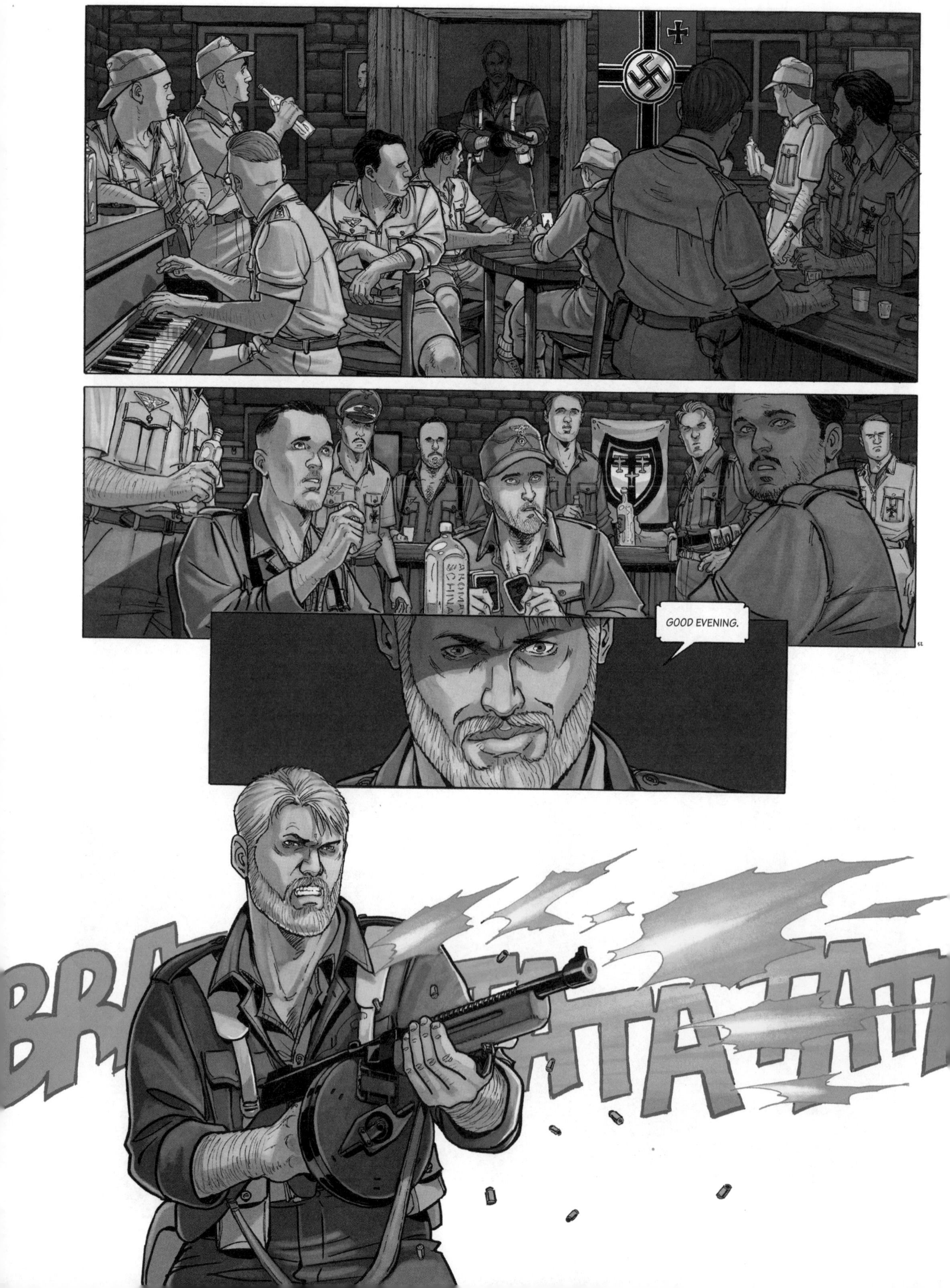
GOOD EVENING.

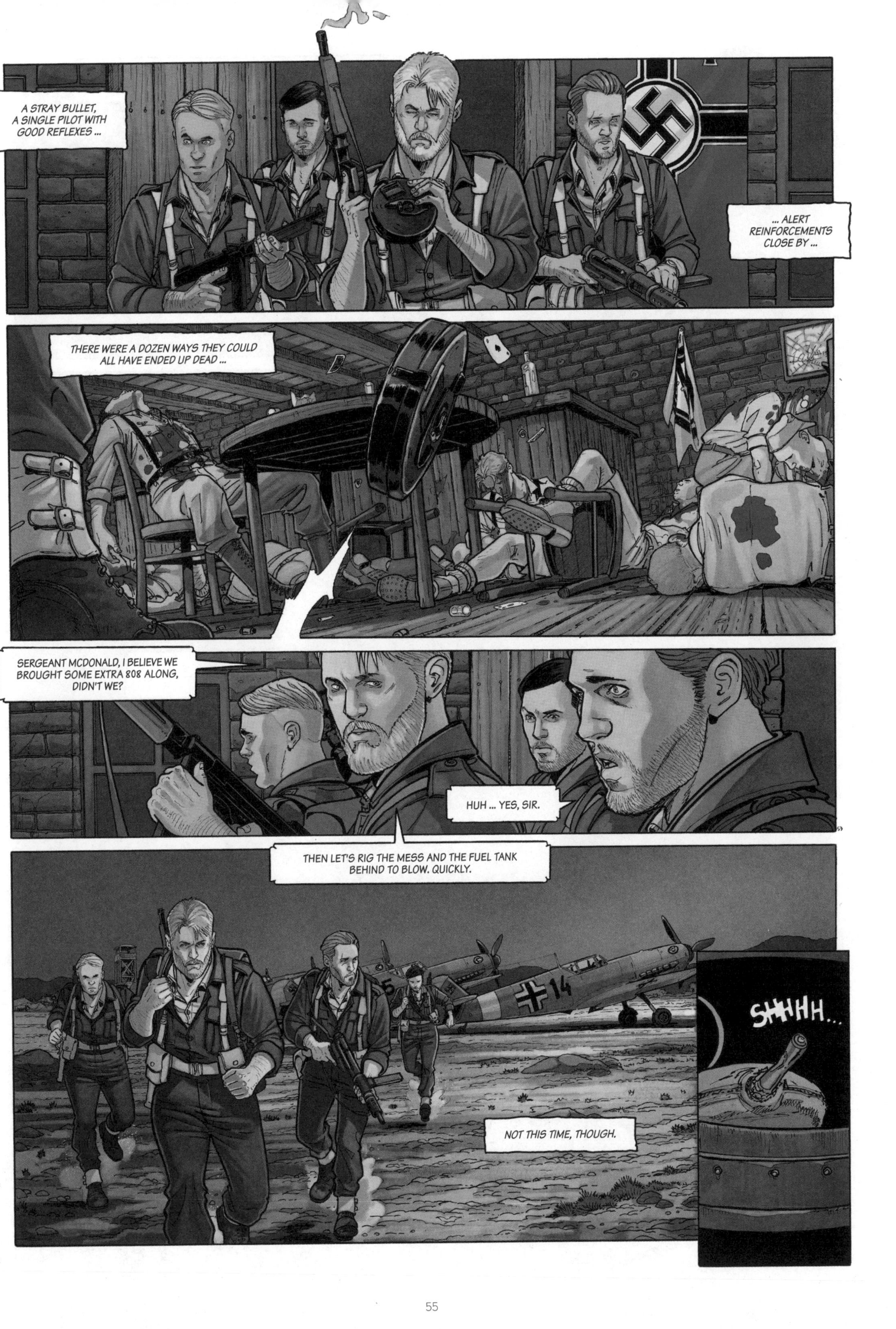
A STRAY BULLET, A SINGLE PILOT WITH GOOD REFLEXES ...
... ALERT REINFORCEMENTS CLOSE BY ...
THERE WERE A DOZEN WAYS THEY COULD ALL HAVE ENDED UP DEAD ...
SERGEANT MCDONALD, I BELIEVE WE BROUGHT SOME EXTRA 808 ALONG, DIDN'T WE?
HUH ... YES, SIR.
THEN LET'S RIG THE MESS AND THE FUEL TANK BEHIND TO BLOW. QUICKLY.
NOT THIS TIME, THOUGH.
SHHHH...

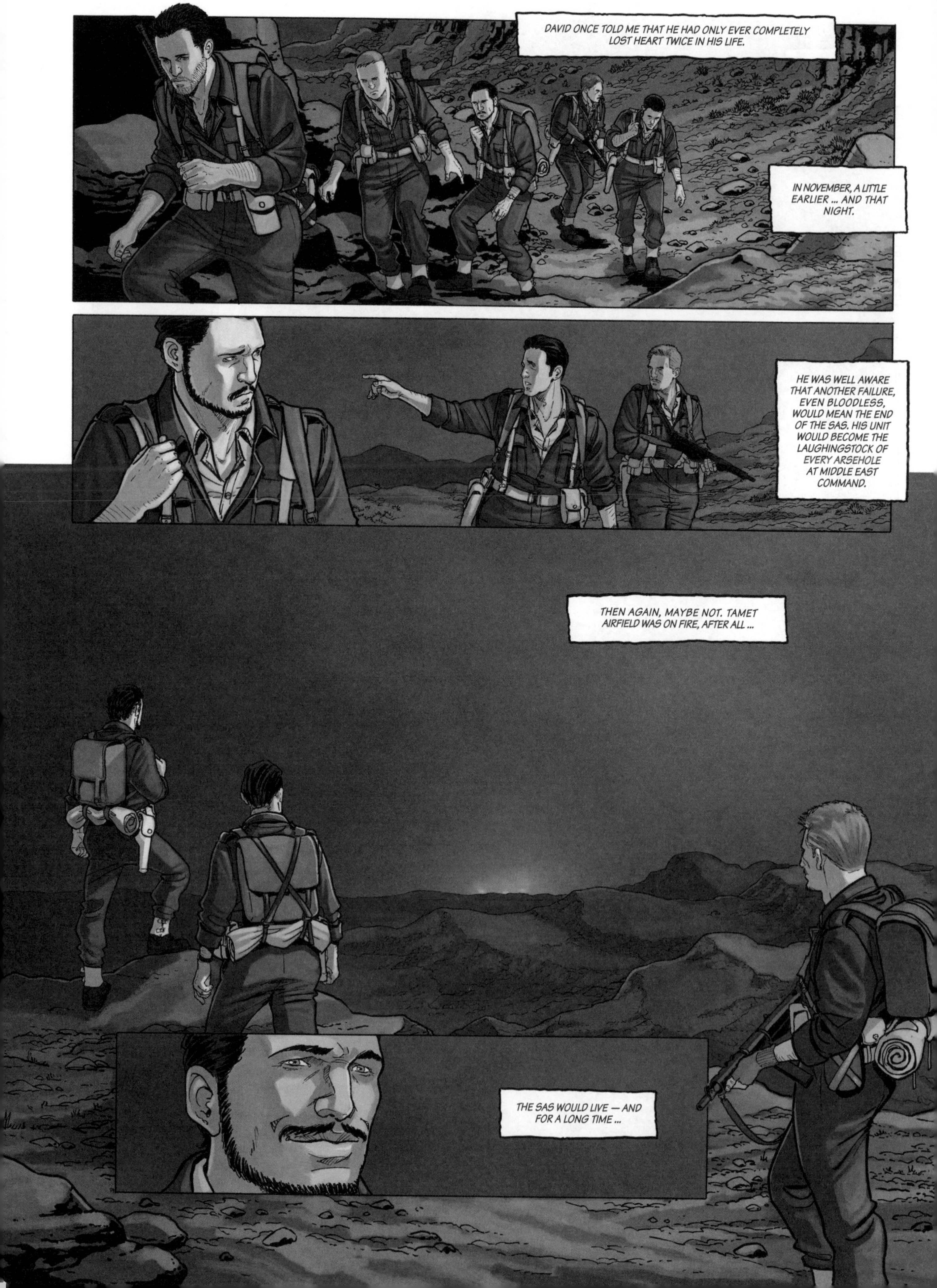
DAVID ONCE TOLD ME THAT HE HAD ONLY EVER COMPLETELY LOST HEART TWICE IN HIS LIFE.
IN NOVEMBER, A LITTLE EARLIER ... AND THAT NIGHT.
HE WAS WELL AWARE THAT ANOTHER FAILURE, EVEN BLOODLESS, WOULD MEAN THE END OF THE SAS. HIS UNIT WOULD BECOME THE LAUGHINGSTOCK OF EVERY ARSEHOLE AT MIDDLE EAST COMMAND.
THEN AGAIN, MAYBE NOT. TAMET AIRFIELD WAS ON FIRE, AFTER ALL ...
THE SAS WOULD LIVE — AND FOR A LONG TIME ...

'Those men are dangerous.
They must be eliminated.
I will hold all commanders
and officers responsible under
military law for any omission
to carry out this order.'

18 October 1942, Adolf Hitler,
speaking of Lieutenant Colonel
Stirling's SAS.

REFERENCES

BOOKS

Eastern Approaches, Fitzroy Maclean

Les commandos SAS dans la Seconde Guerre mondiale,
Christophe Prime

Une histoire des forces spéciales,
Jean-Dominique Merchet

COMICS

The Scorpions of the Desert, Hugo Pratt

SONGS

Song on page 25: *Australia's on the Wallaby*
Traditional Australian

Songs on pages 52-53: *Ein Heller und ein Batzen,
Ich bin der Doktor Eisenbart,* Traditional German

FILMS

Raid on Rommel, Henry Hathaway, 1971

Play dirty, André de Toth, 1969

Sea of Sand, Guy Green, 1958

Un taxi pour Tobrouk, Denys de La Patellière, 1961

VIDEO GAMES

Battlefield 2, Electronic Arts, 2005

Call of Duty, Activision, 2003-2016

Hidden and dangerous, Illusion Softworks, 1999

Medal of Honor, Electronic Arts, 1999-2012

INTRODUCTION

June 1941. Europe was entirely occupied by the Third Reich. Well, not entirely. One island still held out against the invaders.

Despite its massive colonial empire and all its dominions, England felt rather alone in this war. As Churchill had predicted, 'There is only one thing worse than fighting with allies, and that is fighting without them'.

In almost two years of war, the list of allies had become dreadfully short. Poland was invaded right away in September 1939, after a lightning-fast three-week campaign. At the end of eight months of the 'Phoney War', Norway was overrun in April 1940. In May/June 1940 it was France, the strongest ally, which collapsed under the tracks of the *Panzerdivisionen*, closely following Belgium and the Netherlands.

In April 1941, German troops seized Greece and the Balkans. British forces were forced to evacuate hurriedly, under constant Luftwaffe bombing, in a Greek version of the Battle of Dunkirk.

However, the British Army bent, but it did not break. Short on men and equipment, it could rely on the discreet support of the United States, despite that nation's neutrality. And, after the Luftwaffe was exhausted during the Battle of Britain (summer 1940), the threat of a ground invasion of the British Isles was lifted for good.

The new battlefield lay outside Europe: in the deserts of Africa, at the gates of Egypt ...

NORTH AFRICA

To support their Italian ally, Rommel and the Afrika Korps landed in Libya. In mere weeks, the German reinforcements stopped the British offensive cold. Commonwealth forces had no choice but to retreat towards Egypt, leaving behind a strong garrison in the port city of Tobruk, which was soon besieged (April 1941). British High Command drew up plans for a relief operation codenamed Crusader. Planned launch date: November 1941. A brand-new commando unit was slated to support the operation by attacking enemy airfields ...

TIMI

FROM THE BEGINNING OF THE SECO

1939

22 MAY	The Pact of Steel is signed in Berlin between Germany and Italy.
23 AUGUST	The German-Soviet Nonaggression Pact is signed in Moscow.
1 SEPTEMBER	At 4:45 AM, Germany attacks Poland without a formal declaration of war. France and the United Kingdom mobilise their armies.
3 SEPTEMBER	The United Kingdom, Australia, New Zealand, and France declare war on Germany. Thus begins the Phoney War.
17 SEPTEMBER	Soviet troops invade Eastern Poland.
28 SEPTEMBER	Poland is occupied.

1940

10 MAY	Winston Churchill is made Prime Minister of the United Kingdom. The German western offensive begins. End of the Phoney War and beginning of the Battle of France.
13 MAY	Winston Churchill gives one of his most famous speeches: 'I have nothing to offer but blood, toil, tears, and sweat'
16 MAY	General Gamelin orders a general retreat of French forces.
24 MAY	French and British forces in Belgium are defeated. Over 300,000 British and French soldiers are evacuated from Dunkirk, but the British have to leave most of their equipment behind on French beaches
10 JUNE	Italy declares war on France and the United Kingdom.
17 JUNE	Marshall Pétain, newly-appointed French Prime Minister, addresses the nation on the radio: 'It is with a heavy heart that I say to you today that the fighting must stop'. Beginning of surrender negotiations. De Gaulle escapes to London.
22 JUNE	Churchill denounces the signing of the armistice between France and Nazi Germany.
10 JULY	The Battle of Britain begins.
28 AUGUST	First night bombing raids on London.

INE

RLD WAR TO NOVEMBER 1941

SEPTEMBER	Italy launches its invasion of Egypt. It's officially a failure as early as 16 September.
3 DECEMBER	British counteroffensive. In eight weeks, Commonwealth troops crush the Italian Army despite numerical inferiority.
	1941
5 JANUARY	Italian defeat at Bardia, Libya.
11 JANUARY	Colonel Jean Colonna d'Ornano of the Free French Forces and Major Clayton of the LRDG carry out a raid on Murzuk, capital of the Fezzan region (Libya), with a hundred men. The operation is a success, but d'Ornano is killed in action.
12 JANUARY	Tobruk (Libya) is captured by British and Australian troops.
19 JANUARY	British offensive against Italian colonies in Eastern Africa (Ethiopia, Eritrea, Somalia).
7 FEBRUARY	The Italian Tenth Army surrenders at Beda Fomm (Libya). The British take 20,000 prisoners, including six generals.
12 FEBRUARY	General Rommel arrives in North Africa.
24 MARCH	First major offensive of the Afrika Korps, which easily retakes El Agheila (Libya) from the British.
31 MARCH	The Afrika Korps attacks the British positions at Mersa Brega (Libya).
4 APRIL	The Germans take Benghazi (Libya).
15 JUNE	Failure of Operation Battleaxe. The British come extremely close to total disaster. They avoid being completely surrounded but lose over half their tanks. The road to Cairo seems wide open to German forces.
22 JUNE	Hitler launches Operation Barbarossa. The Wehrmacht invades the USSR.
NOVEMBER	Operation Crusader – an offensive aimed at taking back the ground lost to the Afrika Korps and relieving Tobruk – is launched.

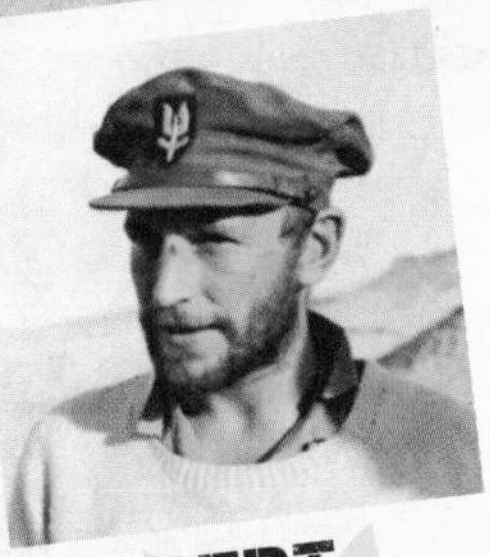

ROBERT « PADDY » BLAIR MAYNE

- Born 11 January 1915 in County Down, Ulster.
- Attended Queen's University of Belfast.
- Became a solicitor.
- Cricketer and golfer, he also practiced precision shooting from an early age.
- Boxer, Irish Universities Heavyweight Champion (1936).
- Professional rugby league player, member of the national Irish squad, then member of the British Lions team on a tour to South Africa (1937-1938).
- At one point during that tour, he brought an antelope back to his hotel room after a teammate complained of the lack of fresh meat.
- Quite fond of strong drink.
- Member of 11 Commando as part of General Robert Laycock's 'Layforce' (1941).

AWARDS: Distinguished Service Order & Three Bars, Légion d'Honneur (France), Croix de Guerre 1939-1945 (France).

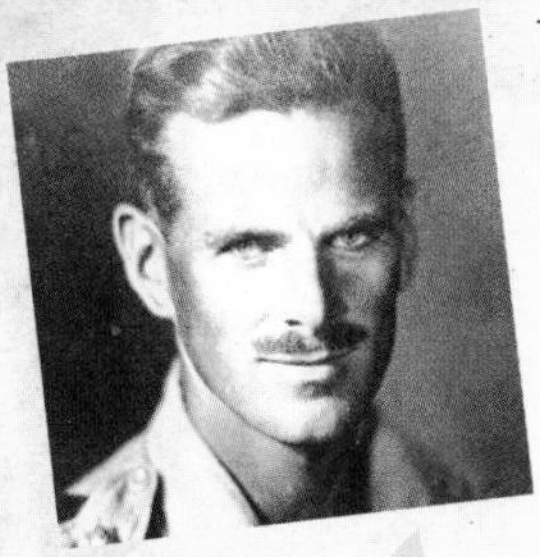

JOHN « JOCK » STEEL LEWES

- Born 21 December 1913, Calcutta; Australian citizen.
- Accomplished sportsman.
- President of the Oxford University Boat Club; his leadership and training ended a 13-year Cambridge winning streak (1937).
- A short stay in Germany opened his eyes to the realities of the Nazi regime.
- Second Lieutenant in the Welsh Guards (1939).
- Member of 8 Commando as part of General Robert Laycock's 'Layforce' (1941).
- Conducted numerous raids behind enemy lines during the siege of Tobruk (1941).
- Designed the incendiary bomb named after him.
- Good-looking, dazzling smile.

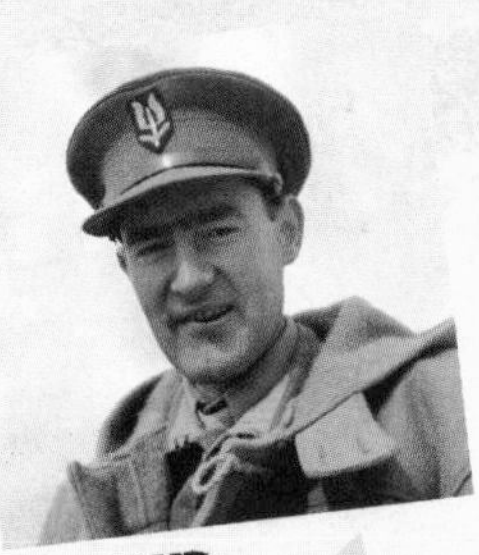

DAVID ARCHIBALD STIRLING

- Born 15 November 1915 in Perthshire, Scotland.
- Expelled from Trinity College at the University of Cambridge following 23 reprimands for unruly behaviour.
- Accomplished sportsman and skilled hiker.
- Second Lieutenant in the supplementary reserves of the Scots Guards (1937).
- Member of 8 Commando as part of General Robert Laycock's 'Layforce' (1941).
- Earned the nickname 'The Phantom Major' following his exploits with the SAS.
- After the war, he founded Watchguard International Ltd., a private military company that employed many former SAS members and worked for British intelligence.
- Regularly worked with MI6.

AWARDS: Knight Bachelor, Distinguished Service Order, Officer of the Order of the British Empire, Légion d'Honneur (France).

LRDG

The story of the Long Range Desert Group began before the war, in Cairo, where adventurers from the Royal Air Force and the Royal Geographic Society met. Under the leadership of Ralph A. Bagnold, those men – explorers and adventurers – would become the greatest desert experts. In order to navigate the great sand sea, they mapped the country and developed a compass – the 'Bagnold Sun Compass'.

During the war, their mission was to spy on and harass Axis forces. They saw little actual combat, but the intelligence they gathered was invaluable; their last exploit in January 1943 was to find a passage through the Mareth Line – a system of fortifications built on the Tunisian border. It allowed the Allies to break through the Line and outflank the Afrika Korps.

Rommel would later pay them homage, saying, 'The Long-Range Desert Group caused us more damage than any other British unit of equal strength'.

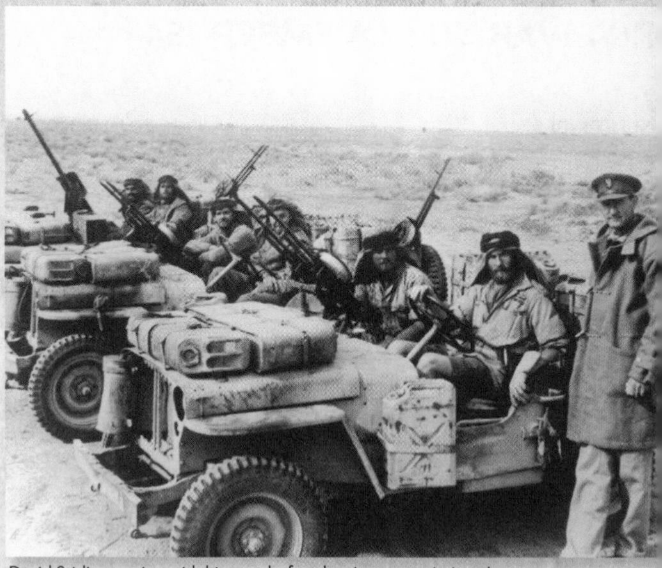

David Stirling posing with his men before leaving on a mission, January 1943

After their collaboration with the LRDG, the SAS would adopt the new American Willys Jeeps. Always eager to tinker and improve, they removed the radiator grill to accelerate cooling and took off the windscreen to clear the way for front- and rear-mounted machine guns.

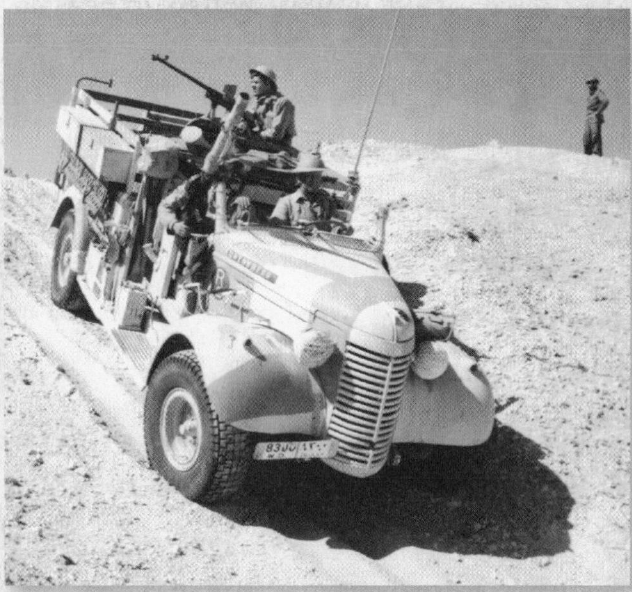

The LRDG troops adopted the British Army Chevrolet WB lorries. They protected the radiators against the sand, designed sand channels and sand mats, and installed extra strong suspensions. They added wireless equipment, machine guns, mortars, and extra storage space for large supplies of fuel and water. Each lorry carried 3,000 pounds of equipment for an operational range of 1,120 miles, enough for extended desert raids.

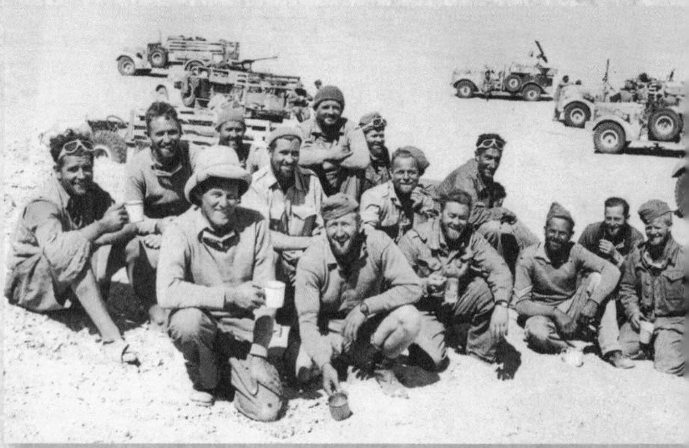

The men Bagnold recruited were, first and foremost, seasoned adventurers, daredevils with a solid knowledge of the desert and intelligence-gathering techniques. Bagnold also recruited wireless operators and navigators able to find their way on the sea of sand. He rounded up his team with multilingual interpreters, necessary to interrogate German and Italian prisoners or converse with the local Arabs.

Those whose paths crossed that of the LRDG were often struck by the troopers' apparel. No standard uniform there but a variety of field uniforms that changed with the time of day – or night. In the evening, when the temperatures fell below zero, it was a thick, padded vest with a woollen hat. Light shirt and shorts in the morning, *keffiyeh* and Bedouin garb to withstand the oppressive heat of midday. The SAS, at first surprised to see them change several times a day, were quick to adopt the same habits.

THE LRDG BADGE

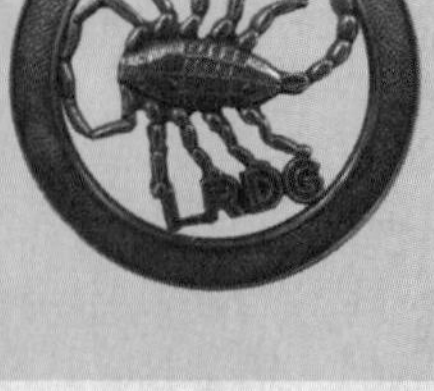

The whole concept of the Long Range Desert Group can be found in this legendary badge. The wheel symbolises the jeeps and lorries used by the group to crisscross the desert. The scorpion is one of the most dangerous creatures of the desert while also perfectly adapted to the extreme weather condition of its natural habitat.

Erwin Rommel (1891-1944)

GENERAL ROMMEL

General Erwin Rommel, promoted to Field Marshall in 1942, was the main opponent of the SAS and the British Army in North Africa between 1941 and 1943. Known as 'the Desert Fox' for his brilliant victories, he long enjoyed a special aura thanks to the legacy of his book *Krieg ohne Haß* (*War without Hate*), as well as his forced suicide in 1944 following the failed assassination attempt on Hitler. However, the latest research has rather overturned this portrait.

A good tactician, he lacked moral perspective and wouldn't hesitate to abandon his troops in trouble. Moreover, Erwin Rommel wasn't the apolitical soldier we believed. Opportunistic and extremely ambitious, he owed everything to Hitler. While not a Nazi fanatic, he represented a loyal, powerful support for the regime. His doubts only appeared when he realised that the war was lost.

THE SAS BADGE

The original SAS insignia was designed by Sergeant Bob Tait around the end of 1941. The dagger is placed at the centre of a crusader shield and surrounded by a pair of wings. The dagger or sword represents the commando's weapon but is also a stylised representation of Excalibur, King Arthur's magic sword.

The wings symbolise the origin of the SAS – parachute units. The design of the wings is borrowed from a pseudo-Egyptian mural in Shepheard's Hotel in Cairo, where Stirling and other officers were billeted; it is a stylisation of those of a sacred ibis. The sky-blue colour is the official colour of the Universities of Oxford and Cambridge, underlining the almost 'aristocratic' origins of the unit's first recruits, who came from the upper class and had quite often received a solid higher education.

The motto, 'Who Dares Wins', exemplifies the spirit of initiative Stirling wanted to inspire in his men. The wings of the French SAS bear the Lorraine cross, symbol of Free France, in the centre below the parachute.

The legacy of the insignia is strong, and a large number of commando units still wear badges designed after it.

THE FOREIGN SAS

Beyond the Rhodesians, New Zealanders, Australians, South Africans, Scots, Irish, Welsh, and English that made up the various SAS squadrons, there were three 'national' squadrons: French, Belgian, and Greek.

THE FRENCH SAS

On 29 September, General de Gaulle created the 1st Air infantry Company. It was made up of 50 of the first and best men to heed his call to resist. Trained in commando techniques and parachuting, those men caught the eye of Stirling, who was looking for new SAS recruits. After North Africa, the French Squadron would be involved in every major operation, notably Brittany, then Belgium and the Netherlands.

By 8 May 1945, only 22 French SAS were left of the 215 who had joined prior to 8 November 1942.

Free French SAS in desert fighter outfits, Tunisia, 1943

THE BELGIAN SAS

5 SAS was made up entirely of Belgian volunteers, who spoke French, Dutch, or English. Created in May 1942, the Belgian SAS carried out their first mission on 28 July 1944. After various operations in Belgium and the Netherlands, in May 1945 they were assigned to hunt down war criminals. Joachim Von Ribbentrop and Alfred Rosenberg are among their most significant collars.

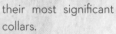

Colonel Blondeel conducting a review of 5 SAS in Brussels after the war

THE GREEK SAS

Created by Colonel Christodoulos Tsigantes, the squadron saw action for the first time in February 1943 in Tunisia, under the command of General Philippe Leclerc. The Greek SAS later took part in numerous operations in the Aegean.

Wilfred Thesiger and Colonel Tsigantes, Libya, 1942

LIBYA

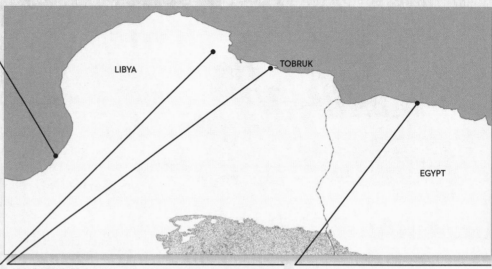

ATTACK ON ADJABIYA
21 December 1941.

OPERATION GREEN ROOM
8 December 1941 (Sirte and Tamet).

ATTACK ON TAMET HARBOUR
24 December 1941.

OPERATION BIGAMY
Late July 1942. Abortive attempt to retake both Benghazi and the Jalo Oasis.

OPERATION SQUATTER
16/17 November 1941 (Gazala).

SIMULTANEOUS ATTACKS ON AL DABA, BAGUSH, FOUKA, AND MERSA MATRUH
5 July 1942.

ATTACK ON SIDI HANEISH AIRFIELD
24 July 1942.

THE SAS FROM 1945 TO TODAY

Since 1945, the SAS have been deployed to several operational theatres and several types of conflicts. They carry out a wide spectrum of missions: intelligence gathering, reconnaissance and surveillance, sabotage and enemy capture, counterterrorism, and the training of foreign troops.

NORTHERN IRELAND
The SAS were embedded in Northern Ireland as early as 1966, under civilian covers first, then in uniform as advisors. Tasked with gathering intelligence and fighting against the IRA, they were accused of carrying out kidnappings and assassinations. Several poorly planned operations led to bloody blunders.

LONDON, OPERATION NIMROD
On 30 April 1980, a group of terrorists took 19 people hostage inside the Iranian embassy. After a five-day siege, the SAS stormed the building, killing five of the hostage-takers and capturing the sixth. This extremely spectacular operation, seen live on TV by millions of Britons, remains one of the unit's most popular feats of arms.

WALES, BRECON BEACONS MOUNTAINS
SAS candidate selection takes place in the Brecon Beacons range in Wales. Extremely demanding, the selection process puts the candidates' mental and physical stamina to the test. By the end of the trials, they will have marched nearly 300 miles carrying their weapons and a 25-kg backpack. Each SAS must be skilled in at least one of the following specialities: field medicine, demolition, linguistics, or signals.

WARS IN YUGOSLAVIA
Several secret infiltration missions took place in former Yugoslavia. Some were aimed at guiding the Coalition's air strikes. After the war, the SAS were assigned to hunt down war criminals.

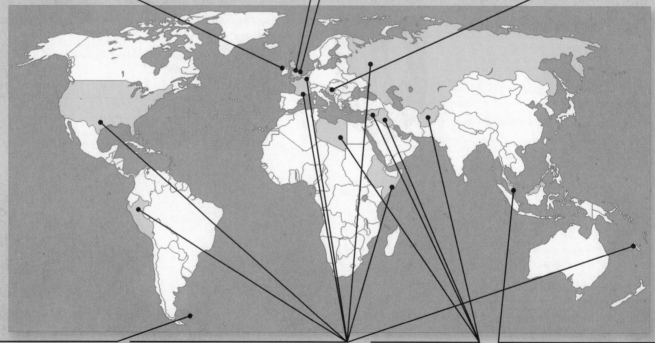

FALKLANDS WAR
Between 2 April and 14 June 1982, war broke out between Argentina and the United Kingdom over ownership of the Falkland Islands. The SAS took a very active part in the fighting. Over 20 lost their lives in the conflict.

ADVISORS
Lima, Moscow, Beslan, Uvea, Waco, the Netherlands, Mogadishu, Marignane ... In many major hostage situations, SAS men were present as advisors or observers. In some cases, as with the hijacking of Lufthansa flight 181, they even took an active part in resolving the crisis.

IRAQ, AFGHANISTAN, SYRIA, LIBYA
As part of the global War on Terror, the SAS conducts an increasing number of intelligence-gathering and/or elimination missions.

MALAYA, 1948-1960
In 1948, several attacks carried out by the Malayan People's Liberation Army pushed the British authority into declaring a state of emergency. In 1950, a group of SAS was deployed there to wage guerrilla warfare in the jungle.

ITALY

The Italian Campaign would be short and frustrating for the SAS. Many of their missions failed because of faulty intelligence, technical problems, or haphazard airdrops. That said, they did take part in the fighting.

MILAN
RIMINI
ROME
PALERMO

OPERATION CANDYTUFT
Over six days, starting from 6 October 1943, several SAS teams destroyed bridges and railways to disorganise the movements of German troops.

OPERATION BAOBAB
In January 1944, an important bridge for the resupplying of German troops was completely destroyed.

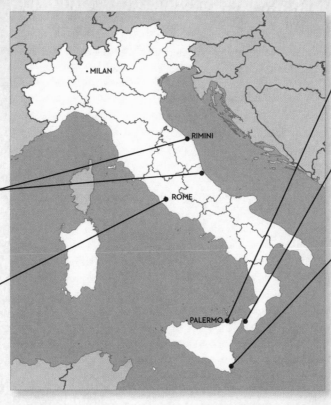

OPERATION CHESTNUT
It was a return to parachute missions for the SAS, but the loss of wireless sets caused the mission to fail.

OPERATION BAYTOWN
Success in Italy at last: the commandos assisted in taking the port of Reggio di Calabria on 3 September 1943.

OPERATION NARCISSUS
The SAS were tasked with taking a lighthouse in order to protect the Allied landings. When they arrived, however, there were no Germans, and they had to pull out without firing a single shot.

FRANCE

From June 1944 on, the SAS saw heavy action in France, most notably the Free French SAS because of their knowledge of local language and culture. As with the other theatres where they fought, the results would vary wildly. Here are six examples among the dozens of operations that took place in France and Northern Europe that year.

CHERBOURG
PARIS
BREST
RENNES
STRASBOURG
CLERMONT-FERRAND

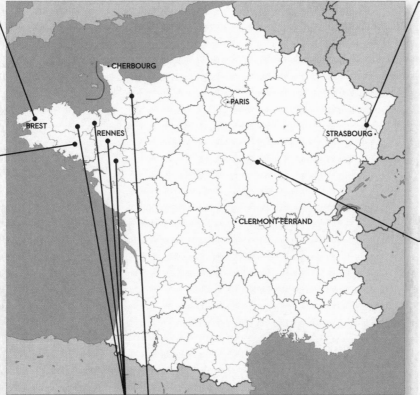

OPERATION DERRY
While the US Army began its push towards the Finistère peninsula, 88 SAS were airdropped during the night of 4 August. Their mission was to protect the bridges that the Allies would need to reach Brest and to help the *maquis* Resistance units that were fighting the Germans.

OPERATION DINGSON
From 6 to 18 June, 160 French SAS were airdropped near Saint-Marcel to set up Dingson Base. But, having become too much of a nuisance, the Saint-Marcel *maquis* were attacked on 18 June by a powerful German force. Dingson was destroyed. The Germans took no prisoners and hunted down the survivors with the help of collaborators. Local civilians, suspected of having sympathy for the Resistance, suffered reprisals.

OPERATION LOYTON
On 12 August, dropped into the heart of the Vosges region, 91 British SAS carried out sabotage and harassment missions to support General Patton's offensive. Betrayed, the SAS were forced into hiding, but the Germans arrested 210 men from the village of Moussey to obtain information. When the villagers refused to talk, though, they were deported. Only 75 would return after the war. Of the SAS, 14 were killed in action, 31 captured and executed.

OPERATION SPENCER
For this operation, 60 heavily armed jeeps were airdropped to the French SAS groups already present in the Loire region. Their role was to protect the southern flank of Patton's army. In the end, several hundred German troops and hundreds of vehicles were put out of action.

OPERATIONS COONEY, GROG, BULBASKET, GAIN, AND DICKENS
Over 20 SAS parachute drops took place between June and August 1944. Most of them were intended for infrastructure sabotage missions (railways, fuel depots, power grids).

OPERATION TITANIC IV
This operation took place the day before D-Day. It was aimed at misleading the Germans with a mass drop of several hundred dummy paratroopers and a few SAS teams. The SAS used recordings of men shouting, guns firing, and even mortars to make it sound like a much bigger air assault.

INTERVIEW

Interview with Jean-Dominique Merchet, journalist and special forces expert. He is the author of *Une histoire des forces spéciales* [*A History of Special Forces*], published by Editions Jacob-Duvernet, and runs the blog www.lopinion.fr/blog/secret-defense.

What was the strategic and tactical usefulness of the SAS during the Second World War?

Honestly, from a strategic standpoint, very limited. We're talking more about pinpricks than major strikes. That said, you have to understand what situation England is in in June/July 1941 when Stirling creates the SAS. In Western Europe, England stands alone against Nazi Germany. The Russians are collapsing out east, the only allies left to the British are often faraway Commonwealth nations (the Americans are still neutral), and after the disaster at Dunkirk, they have no equipment either. To counter the threat, all that is left to them are bombing campaigns against Germany – but they don't have the right airplanes yet. They hold against the Luftwaffe during the Battle of Britain, but that's about it. In that summer of 1941, Egypt is clearly threatened by the Italians and Rommel's troops. If Egypt falls, all of the Middle East is threatened. Besides, Egypt is one of the empire's crown jewels. Letting it fall to the Nazis is inconceivable. The British will do everything they can to hold out, and a fair number of 'nutters' will try to put together screwball units. A lot were recorded all over the place, from Norway to Greece. Very few will survive long, and the SAS will be the only ones to know such posterity.

What are the advantages of such units?

Well, the country is led by a magnificent 'nutter'. Churchill isn't fettered by the squeamishness of traditional military minds and is willing to study any project if it can benefit the nation. So the first interest is a practical one: the British will go all in. Also, such small units come pretty cheap, which is important. It's not something the legend ever mentions, but it's an important argument for High Command. They use very light, inexpensive equipment. In some cases – including the SAS themselves – they even steal from other regiments to equip themselves. Finally, many of the SAS soldiers aren't suitable material for regular armies. They're aggressive, undisciplined, hard to control. The brass feel better having them outside of traditional chains of command.

How do they go about delivering those pinpricks?

On the ground, those men cannot conduct large-scale operations. So they'll sting the enemy, anger him. While such actions cannot win battles, and even less so the war, their mode of action forces their opponents to remain alert, to tie up large contingents to guard installations and airfields. Over the whole of the Eastern Mediterranean theatre, that represents a considerable number of soldiers. Another aspect is that they don't really have any traditional military training. They're built for lightning-fast raids. But

very often, those raids fail, and a lot of missions are complete debacles, such as the SAS's first parachute mission, which turned into a disaster because of a lack of caution and common sense. Same thing in Saint-Marcel, Brittany, and Verrières, Burgundy, in 1944. The SAS were careless and let the *maquis* grow too large, too visible. The Germans couldn't overlook it, and in both cases it ended in bloody disaster.

What has the SAS invented?

Nothing, really. There have always been commandos and irregular units. What sets them apart is that they do not follow the chivalric rules of war. They don't do things nobly – if that notion even means anything in war. They prefer shrewdness to strength, raiding to pitched battles with artillery, infantry, and cavalry. They will turn that spirit into a strength and a way to forge a legend.

They did invent one thing, though, and that's the four-man team – something that's now in general use everywhere. They found out that four is the right number – as three means two against one and five becomes too many, requiring too many logistics.

What services based themselves on the SAS after the war? Do they have successors?

The only successors to Stirling's SAS are the current British, Australian, and New Zealand SAS. They remain the best, the most effective special services. Other nations have units that resemble them, but the military and intelligence cultures unique to each mean profound differences that make comparisons impossible. In France, they could be likened to the RPIMa or the Dragons Parachutistes. As a matter of fact, during the Algerian War, several former SAS were members of those units. The Russians and the Israelis are also very different. The American SEALs are a lot more brutal – they're more killers than commandos. America's Green Berets have some things in common, but only some.

What have the SAS been used for since the war?

For a long time they were deployed on counterinsurgency missions, for instance in Malaya or Ireland, where they remained for 30 years. They performed their traditional role during the Falklands War. Currently they've specialised in counterterrorism. They're known to be present in Iraq, Afghanistan, Libya, and Syria. They gather intelligence and eliminate terrorists. Details are rather difficult to ascertain with precision, as there are very few SAS. British papers mention them from time to time, but there's a lot of fantasy and little actual info.